William Shakespeare

The True Story of Life about Great William Shakespeare

(A Life from Beginning an Intimate Look into the Life of the Most Brilliant Writer)

Johnny Perry

Published By **Darby Connor**

Johnny Perry

All Rights Reserved

William Shakespeare: The True Story of Life about Great William Shakespeare (A Life from Beginning an Intimate Look into the Life of the Most Brilliant Writer)

ISBN 978-0-9938088-1-4

No part of this guidebook shall be reproduced in any form without permission in writing from the publisher except in the case of brief quotations embodied in critical articles or reviews.

Legal & Disclaimer

The information contained in this book is not designed to replace or take the place of any form of medicine or professional medical advice. The information in this book has been provided for educational & entertainment purposes only.

The information contained in this book has been compiled from sources deemed reliable, and it is accurate to the best of the Author's knowledge; however, the Author cannot guarantee its accuracy and validity and cannot be held liable for any errors or omissions. Changes are periodically made to this book. You must consult your doctor or get professional medical advice before using any of the suggested remedies, techniques, or information in this book.

Upon using the information contained in this book, you agree to hold harmless the Author from and against any damages, costs, and expenses, including any legal fees potentially resulting from the application of any of the information provided by this guide. This disclaimer applies to any damages or injury caused by the use and application, whether directly or indirectly, of any advice or information presented, whether for breach of contract, tort, negligence, personal injury, criminal intent, or under any other cause of action.

You agree to accept all risks of using the information presented inside this book. You need to consult a professional medical practitioner in order to ensure you are both able and healthy enough to participate in this program.

Table Of Contents

Chapter 1: The Essence Of William Shakespeare 1

Chapter 2: His Poetry And Drama 20

Chapter 3: His Plays 32

Chapter 4: The Middle Years Plays 54

Chapter 5: William Shakespeare 103

Chapter 6: The Funerary Shakespeare Monument, Holy Trinity Church, Stratford 112

Chapter 7: William Shakespeare Hated To Feel Life 132

Chapter 8: The Fatal Legs Of The Two Enemies 147

Chapter 9: His Entire Life 172

Chapter 10: Evolution In The Poetry 1592-1595 180

Chapter 1: The Essence Of William Shakespeare

William Shakespeare, whose name can be pronounced "Shakspere," byname Bard of Avon or Swan of Avon, (who was baptized on 26 April 1564 at Stratford-upon-Avon, Warwickshire, England) was an English actor, poet and performer who is often called"the" English country poet, and regarded by many to be the finest actor of all time.

Shakespeare occupies a unique position in literature from all over the world. Other poets like Homer and Dante writers, such as Leo Tolstoy and Charles Dickens are able to transcend boundaries of the country, but the track records of any author compares to the one of Shakespeare and his plays composed during the 16th century and the early 17th century for the sake of a small performance theatre they are frequently performed and by more people in more countries than at any time in the past. The prediction made by Shakespeare's amazing contemporary, the writer and poet Ben Jonson, that Shakespeare "was not of an age, but for perpetuity," is now a reality.

It could be a bit risky trying to find a meaningful meaning for his accomplishment, however it's easy to identify the qualities which allowed him to create imaginative visions of pathos and comedy that, whether they are read or viewed in the theatre, fill the intellect and brain and stay in the brain. The author has extraordinary intellectual speed, perceptiveness and poetry. Some authors possess the same qualities, however with Shakespeare his mind's zeal was not applied to obscure and distant subjects, but instead human beings and their entire diversity of thoughts and conflicts. Some authors have utilized their mind's zeal in the same way, however Shakespeare is extremely adept with pictures and words, which means that his mental energy used in a way that is understandable to human conditions, can be expressed in a incredible and dazzling expression. engaging and imaginatively advocating. In case this weren't enough to be said, the genre in which his ideas were channeled wasn't a bookish and remote form however, it was a vibrant performance of actors that evoked empathy and the audience to participate in his character. Thus, the benefits of Shakespeare's work can be translated to different languages and societies that are different from Elizabethan England.

While the amount of precise information on Shakespeare is staggeringly large for an individual of his position in the world, some are a bit dissatisfied since it's mostly collected from documents of the major actor. Dates of baptisms and marriage relations, deaths, burials; wills and conveyances or legal proceedings, as well as settlements by the courtsthose are the dirty details. However, there are numerous modern allusions of his writing which provide a substantial amount of blood and flesh to the biographical skull.

Early Life in Stratford

The register of the parish at Holy Trinity Church in Stratford-upon-Avon, Warwickshire, shows that the baptism took place on the 26th of April 1564. His birthday was usually celebrated on the 23rd of April. His father, John Shakespeare, was an enrolled citizen in the district. In 1565 was elected to be an alderman. In 1568, he was also a bailiff (the post of mayor prior to the granting another charter in Stratford on 1664). He was involved in various types of commerce and is believed to have had some shifts with regard to his performance. His wife, Mary Arden, of Wilmcote, Warwickshire, originated from an old family, and was also the heir to a certain properties.

Stratford was awed by a grade school with good standards, and their education was for free, with and the wages of the schoolmaster were paid to the school district. The lists of pupils who attended the school during the 16th century are still in existence, but it's absurd to think that bailiffs of the town did not take his child to the school. The school's curriculum would comprise mostly of Latin research-based studies, studying to write, read, and converse in the language proficiently and taking classes with the Classical philosophers, historians, and authors. Shakespeare did not go to the university and it's unlikely that his academic course of argumentation, oratory as well as other studies that were conducted there would have been of interest to Shakespeare.

At the age of 18, He got married at age 18. When and where remains unknown, but the registry of the episcopal church in Worcester has a bond that was issued on 28 November 1582 which was executed by two ladies from Stratford known as Sandells and Richardson in order to provide a security for the bishop to resolve an issue with a license for the wedding of William Shakespeare and "Anne Hathaway of Stratford," upon the consent of her good family and friends, as well as on a request to be granted the banns. (Anne died in 1623, only 7 years later than Shakespeare. There is evidence to connect her with a clan of Hathaways who lived in a stunning farmhouse that is now well cleaned out, just about 2 miles far from Stratford.) The following date of significance can be found in the archives from the Stratford church where a baby girl, named Susanna was born to William Shakespeare, was baptized on the 26th of May 1583. On February 2nd 1585, two twins were baptized: Hamnet as well as Judith. (Hamnet the Shakespeare's only child, was killed one year later).

The way in which Shakespeare went about the remaining 8 years of his existence, until his name begins appearing in London the theater's archives, isn't fully understood. There are tales which were subsequently used as currency death -- of taking deer, and getting into troubles with a regional mogul Sir Thomas Lucy of Charlecote, close to Stratford as well as of earning his income as a schoolmaster across the United States; of relocating to London and gaining access to the theater world by taking care of the horses of people who attended the theater and also spectators. There is also speculation that Shakespeare had a brief period of time as a part of a prestigious home, and was also an officer, perhaps during one of the Low Nations. Instead of relying on external evidence these projections of Shakespeare's life are usually constructed by analyzing an inside "proof" of his works. This method, however, cannot be accepted: one is unable to find out, for instance the insinuations he made about his lawful authority the fact that Shakespeare is an attorney since he was clearly an writer who was able to obtain any information he required to create the structures of his play.

His Personal Life

Shakespeare did not have any interaction with the bureaucracy. The only contact was wearing the royal livery of one of the King's Men-- at the crowning ceremony of James I in 1604. James I in 1604.

Shakespeare continued to take look after his monetary needs. He acquired houses in London and Stratford. In 1605 he was granted an amount (about 1/5th) of Stratford the tithes-- an occurrence that explains the reason his burial took place inside the chancel of the church. A short period of time, the family he was staying with were the French Huguenot family, known as Mountjoy which was located near St. Olave's Church in Cripplegate, London. There are records of a dispute from May 1612, which arose out of an Mountjoy family feud, depict Shakespeare to have presented his case by demonstrating his charm (though incapable of recalling the crucial details that could be the basis of the dispute) and also for being interested generally in family matters.

None of the letters written by Shakespeare are in circulation however a letter written by him to him was outstripped by some major transactions of the city of Stratford which is why it has been preserved in the archives of the district. The letter was written by Richard Quiney and dealt with by him in his residence at Bell Inn in Carter Lane, London, whither he was going to Stratford to conduct business. On the reverse of the document is written: "To my loving buddy and compatriot, Mr. Wm. Shakespeare, provide these." Evidently Quiney considered the colleague Stratfordian one who he could ask for a loan of L 30-which was an amount that was substantial in Elizabethan the era. There isn't much more to know much about the exchange however, since so very few opportunities of getting a glimpse the personal lives of Shakespeare exist, the pleading note ends up becoming an incredibly touching document. The letter is interesting in that, after 18 years, Quiney's son Thomas became the wife of Judith Shakespeare's 2nd daughter.

Shakespeare's will (made on March 25 1616) is a lengthy and intricate dossier. It outlines his fairly adequate assets on male siblings of his elder daughter Susanna. (Both the girls were later married, one to the above mentioned Thomas Quiney and the other to John Hall, a highly respected doctor from Stratford.) In a remark that he would bestow the "second-best bed" to his wedding partner, but no one can determine what this famous practice signifies. The testator's signatures on the will appear to be on the wrong side of his hand. It is possible that Shakespeare was already sick. Shakespeare died on April 23, 1616. There was no name written on the gravestone of his within the church's chancel in the church of parish in Stratford-upon-Avon.

In the age of 18 in 1582, the couple got married Anne Hathaway, a woman that was eight years older than him. Their first child, Susanna, was born on the 26th of May 1583. This was six months following the wedding. The license was issued for the wedding on November 27th of 1582. It contained just one reading (rather rather than the standard three) of the banns or declaration of intent to marry, to allow anyone the opportunity to voice any legal issues. The speedy delivery of the couple's baby suggests that the baby wasn't planned and was clearly premarital. This marriage appears to be an "shotgun" wedding event. Anne gave birth 21 months after the birth of Susanna twins. They were named Hamnet and Judith Christening took place on February 2nd 1585. Then William and Anne had children. They married up to the time of his death in 1616. Is this to impress or did they remain loving the other? The historians are left with several questions, that unfortunately, are unanswered.

Did they meet the criteria to be able to live together? Or were they not? Or did William prefer living separately from Anne throughout the period? If he moved to London sometime between 1585 and 1592 it was the first time he took his family to London with the move. The idea of divorce was not so realistic at this time. Are there any health-related or other factors that contributed to the absence of any children? Did he live in Stratford at the time that Hamnet was his sole child who died in 1596 aged eleven? He bought a beautiful residence for his family at Stratford and also acquired real estate within the region. The final resting place was Holy Trinity Church in Stratford which is where Anne came to join him in 1623. It appears that he had moved from Stratford from London in 1612 or so. He lived in a separate house from his family and wife and children, with perhaps occasional visits during the course of his hectic professional career and for at minimum of twenty years. The bequest he left in his final will and a declaration of the "2nd best bed" to Anne with no further mention to her name in the document, suggests to a lot of academics that this marriage was the result of dissatisfaction caused by a sudden childbirth.

In a note dated 13 March 1602 in the popular journal of a law school student named John Manningham, Shakespeare had one of his most memorable experiences when his ears were stung by someone female at the performance in the midst of Richard III making an assignation together with Richard Burbage, the leading actor of which Shakespeare was also a part of. In the midst of heard their conversation,

Shakespeare apparently accelerated to the location where the assignment was set and found himself "amused" by the woman as well as "at his game" when Burbage came in. After a signal was received by a person who claimed that "Richard the Third" had been seen, Shakespeare is supposed to be the one who "triggered the return of Richard the Third to show to show that William the Conqueror had been prior to Richard the Third. Shakespeare's name was William." The diary entry by Manningham should be considered with suspicion because it's not supported without any other evidence and because it may speak to the timeless fact that the stars are regarded to be bohemians and free spirits. The story was so captivating that it was repeated as well as decorated and published by Thomas Loves in his A General View of the Stage (1759) prior to the time that Manningham's journals were discovered.

This does at minimum suggest, to some extent the possibility that Manningham believed it was the case the fact that Shakespeare was heterosexual, and therefore not opposed to occasional affair with his wedding vows. The film Shakespeare in Love (1998) is a fun way to play with this notion through its fictitious discussion about Shakespeare's romantic affair with a woman named Viola Lesseps. She hoped to be an athlete in an elite acting troupe and was the one who inspired Shakespeare to write Romeo and Julietas well as providing him with the best lines.

In addition to these attractive scenarios, no proof can make an impact on poetry and plays Shakespeare composed. What can we learn from these works? Sonnets that were written in a long time span beginning in the 1590s and continuing into the 1660s, document an intensely loving relationship between the person who wrote the sonnets as well as a young boy. At times, the poet is constant and is surrounded by the love which appears reciprocal. In more frequent instances, the love relationship is a struggle because of painfully bare gaps, feelings of jealousy, by the poet's view that other writers are gaining the love of his boy in the end, and then by the utter despair of a blatant defiance where the boy takes the poet's beauty whose sexual gratifications have been enjoyed by the poet in (though it's not without a resentment of his unchecked sexual desire like in Sonnet 130). The story seems to suggest heterosexual love within the poet-speaker regardless of whether it's a struggle and guilty type; however, does the previous sonnets hint at that there is a love for the boy? It is suggested that the relationship is surely a reliant and psychological relationship and the poet cannot live without his friend and that friend's willingness to return his love for the poet he deeply feels. But readers can't determine if that love is aimed at physical fulfillment. Absolutely, Sonnet twenty challenges this possibility by insisting that Nature has set up to the perfect friend "just one thing to my purpose absolutely nothing"--the word "penis" penis. This implies that sexual intimacy must be considered to be exclusively the domain of the woman's friendship with the good friend: "However since she [Nature] punctured thee out for women's enjoyment,/ Mine be thy love and thy love's use their treasure." A witty reference to "punctured" highlights the sexual significance of the sonnet's final couplet. The critic Joseph Pequigney has argued at long length that sonnets respect a physical connection between the poet and the friend who is a good one

However, many scholars have been reluctant to accept this kind of assertion.

The biggest issue is that it's impossible to ensure that the sonnets have a personal story behind them. Shakespeare is such an adept actor that it is easy to imagine him coming up with captivating plots that would be the base for his sonnet collection. Then is the order in which the sonnets were printed in the manner that Shakespeare could have wanted to? It appears that he has not had any connection with the publication in 1609 - many years after the bulk of them were written. But, you can consider why a tale like this could have attracted Shakespeare. Are there any levels that dreamwork and dreams can be integrated?

Chapter 2: His Poetry And Drama

Shakespeare was born in a where concepts and ideas and social systems created in the Middle Ages still notified human thinking and behaviour. The Queen Elizabeth I served as God's aide throughout the world. the lords and people were given their rightful place as part of the civilized world under her. and responsibilities that extended up to God as well as the lower ranks. This order however, was not unquestioned. It was believed that theism was untrue to the beliefs and way of life of Elizabethans However, the Christian belief system did not remain a singular belief. Rome's authority was challenged with Martin Luther, John Calvin as well as a multitude of minor spiritual communities, and most importantly the English church in its own right. It was the royal authority that was challenged by Parliament. The financial and social order was shattered with the advent of commercialism as well as the restructuring of properties and plots that were aristocratic during the reign of Henry VIII, and by the rise of education as well as the rise in wealth due to the discovering colonies.

The interaction between new concepts and older ones was common in the past: principal sermons urged people to obedient behavior; Italian politician Niccolo Machiavelli was stating a novel, practical political code that caused Englishmen to be wary of his Italian "Machiavillain" and yet they were prompted to inquire about the men what they did in contrast to what they were required to be doing. In Hamlet Disquisitions-about man, faith and belief, the "rotten" state, and instances of "out of joint"-clearly show the increasing skepticism and dismay. Translations of the Montaigne Essays in 1603 added value, variation and rigor to this thinking in the 1603 edition, and Shakespeare was one of several who read them giving direct and significant quotations within The Tempest. In the philosophical realm, the query "How?" became the motivation to advance rather than the traditional "Why?" that was the hallmark of Aristotle. Shakespeare's plays that were written between 1603-1606 demonstrate a new Jacobean distrust. James I, who, similar to Elizabeth was a great authority but was much less capable than Elizabeth to keep the supreme authority on the throne. The known as Gunpowder Plot (1605) revealed a certain difficulty for only a small portion of the country; James's fights against the home of Commons during the subsequent Parliaments and also displaying that he was a strong leader among James I, the "new guys," also highlighted the shortcomings of the government.

Poetic Conventions and Remarkable Customs

The Latin comedy works from Plautus and Terence were a part of Elizabethan colleges and universities in the Elizabethan schools and universities, as well as English adaptations or translations of these were performed regularly by students. Seneca's dramatic, witty and thought-provoking dramas, too, were translated and often copied. There was another strong local remarkable tradition that was rooted in the Middle Ages playwrights, that continued to be staged across different cities until it was banned in the Elizabethan rule. It was a local drama that been able to perform into French popular farces as well as morality plays influenced by the clerical system with abstract themes, as well as short home entertainments which utilized"the "turns" of individual clowns and actors. The immediate precursors of Shakespeare's plays were often referred to as University Wits, their works weren't arranged in the manner of what they studied during their time at Oxford or Cambridge and instead utilized and developed popular narrative styles.

The English language in the present is evolving and expanding its range. It was the poet Edmund Spenser led with the restoration of old words as well as schoolmasters, writers modern flatterers, and even tourists have all contributed more in France, Italy, and the Roman classics as well as from further away. Aided by the access to cheaper, printed publications and printed books, the language began to become standard with respect to grammar and vocabulary as well as slowly, also with regard to spelling. Affirming an European as well as irreversible credibility, the writer and philosopher Francis Bacon wrote in Latin and in English However in the event that he been alive a couple of decades further on, he could feel confident about his native tongue.

Shakespeare's Literary Financial Obligations

The most obvious financial debt of Shakespeare was due to Raphael Holinshed, whose Chronicles (the 2nd edition that was published in 1587) provided story ideas for several plays. This include Macbeth as well as King Lear. The early Shakespeare works also have there are other debts that stand out evidently for the following reasons: Plautus for the design in The Comedy of Errors; to the poet Ovid as well as to Seneca to the author of oratory and events in Titus Andronicus as well as to ethics drama, for an action where a father is grieving the death of his son and also a boy who was his father to mourn his dead father as in Henry VI, Part 3 as well as for Christopher Marlowe for beliefs and the characterisation of Richard III and The Merchant of Venice and to the Italian popular tradition of commedia dell'arte to distinguish style and classification for the play The Taming of the Shrew and The Taming of the Shrew; etc. In the middle, however it was impossible to discern a line between his results and their. The play "The Tempest" (maybe the most innovative of his plays with regard to structure, style, theme and set) folk-inspired influences can be discerned. This is in addition to the more recent and obvious ties to a formal disguise, which was developed in the late 19th century by Ben Jonson and others at the Court of James the King. James.

The last work of Shakespeare's, Cardenio (now lost) is most likely to be based on certain events, including Cardenio of Miguel de Cervantes' work Don Quixote. As the great play was transliterated to English during 1612 through Thomas Shelton, it was immediately available to Shakespeare as well as John Fletcher when they obviously joined forces as the writers of Cardenio during 1613. Fletcher made use of Cervantes for a number of his plays later on.

Theatrical Conditions of William Shakespeare

The World as well as it's predecessor, the Theatre was a public theatre houses operated under the Chamberlain's Men, a leading theatre company, of which Shakespeare was one of the members. Practically everyone of all classes with the exception of a few Puritans as well as like-minded Reformers visited their homes for afternoon entertainment. They were also called for court appearances, performing before the king as well as the crowds of nobility. If they were in a state of distress typically in summer they would travel to the regions occasionally, and they would perform at the in London's Inns of Court (associations of law students) and at university, as well as in grand homes. The appeal created a need for theater: as early as 1613, the King's Men-- as they were referred to as the Chamberlain's Men were then knownas at the time -- were allowed to perform "fourteen some plays." It quickly became becoming fashionable from 1608 toin 1608-09 the King's Men began to perform regularly at Blackfriars the Blackfriars, which was the Blackfriars, a "personal" indoor theater where fees for admission were high, giving that the organization could attract a larger and sophisticated public for their shows.

Shakespeare's first encounters with his fellow actors in the Chamberlain's Men appear to have been in the form of a show. It is not known if he been in the theater after 1603; and in the custom of his time, he was given only small roles such as the ghost from Hamlet as well as Adam as in As You Like It, however his continual association with them has given him a complete knowledge of all elements of the theater.

The majority of his plays express a consideration for the theater and the responses of the audience.

Hamlet offers expert direction to becoming top performers in the art acting. Prospero In The Tempest mentions the entirety of human existence as a kind of "revels," or theatrical spectacle, that, much as a dream, can rapidly end. In Richard II, the Duke of York in Richard II knows the importance of

... at a theatre, the gaze of men

A well-honored actor departs the scene Idly swayed on who comes next.

The thought of his rantings being monotonous.

The time of Shakespeare was when there was no time to hold group rehearsals in which actors received the lines of their respective roles.

The most important scenes of Shakespeare's plays for this reason, have between two or three characters, in the event that there is an individual character who is able to control a busy stage.

The majority of roles for women were written by younger male actors or for males, and so Shakespeare didn't often write large parts for women or maintain their interest during long stages.

Playing for the clowns of the company-who were among the most well-known attraction in every play-- presented the challenge of giving them the ability to utilize their characters, tricks and comical personalities while still serving their immediate interests in themes and actions.

Chapter 3: His Plays

Let's discuss the most well-known Shakespeare productions.

The Earlier Plays

Shakespeare appeared in London probably sometime in the 1580s in the latter half of the century. The actor was late 20s. The details of when he first began his career in the theatre or what actors he composed the first plays, which can be difficult to identify. In a way, they suggest a period of training and training, the plays show closer resemblance London actors of the 1580s as well as to Classical models than later work. The writer learned how to write plays through a resemblance to the accomplishments of the London theater, which is what anyone who is a young poet or budding theater actor would be able to do.

Titus Andronicus

Titus Andronicus (c. 1589- Titus Andronicus (c. 1589--) is an excellent case of this. It was Shakespeare's first complete-length drama the play owes its major part of its structure, theme and style the work of Thomas Kyd's The Spanish Catastrophe, which proved to be a major achievement in the 1580s. Kyd discovered the idea of adapting the dramatic style of Seneca (the older) and the legendary Stoic stateman and thinker in response to the requirements of a thriving new London theatre.

It resulted in the vengeance drama, an extremely effective genre that would later be reinvented in Hamlet and a host of other revenge plays. Shakespeare took a page from his modern master Christopher Marlowe. The Vice-like character in Marlowe's The Jew of Malta, Barabas might have influenced Shakespeare when he portrayed the vile Aaron The Moor of Titus Andronicus however, others Vice character types were easily accessible to him, too.

The Senecan model could be described as Kyd the opportunity to write Shakespeare told a story of bloody revenge that was triggered in the beginning by a murder or the rape of a person who's family members (dads or brothers, sons) are bound by an oath of spiritual swearing to take revenge for the atrocity.

The person who is retaliated against must proceed by taking care and prudence, since his adversary is clever as well as deceiving. The aggressor ends up becoming insane or fakes being insane to disguise his intentions. In the end, he becomes self-conscious in the process of pursuing his aim of getting revenge. But at the same time, the man is hesitant, and concerned by moral aspects to take into consideration. The vengeance value is contrary to Christian forgiveness. Avenging might be able to see his own spirit in the individual who died in a wrong way that he must take revenge for. The device he uses is an act inside the game to accomplish his goals. The drama ends in bloodshed and an affirmation of the villain. In this play is the tale of Titus andronicus who's sons are killed and whose daughter is tortured and cut up, as well as the tragic story of Hamlet as well as other characters.

The Early Romantic Comedy Plays

Apart from Titus andronicus, Shakespeare was not a fan of official tragedies during his first years. (Though Shakespeare's

English dramas of the historical period were about terrible incidents however, the focus of their work was on something else.) The playwright's young age led him more quickly into comedy and he had greater success immediately. His models are dramatic actors Robert Greene and John Lyly along with Thomas Nashe. This results in a genre that is which is easily and clearly Shakespearean although the actor learned in his studies of Greene and Lyly. The result is a romantic comedy. Similar to the works of Shakespeare's models, his comedy early plays are filled with stories of amorous courtships where an enthralling and extraordinary girl (played by a boy actor) will be paired up against her male lover. Julia is one of two young heroines of The 2 Gentlemen of Verona (c. 1590- 1494) She disguises herself to appear as a male to follow her lover Proteus who is sent to Verona for Milan. Proteus (properly called the adaptable

Proteus from Greek myth) is, as she discovers, has been paying too all focus on Sylvia her precious Proteus's friend, Valentine. Friendship and love therefore battle for the separate vows of the unfaithful male until the love of his partner and the unending chaste devotion of both women restore Proteus back to the right path. The concept of a girl disguised as a man was significant for Shakespeare when he wrote his romantic comedy dramas including The Merchant of Venice, As You Like It, and Twelfth Night. Similar to the way that it is with Shakespeare He derived the basic plot from the narrative of a story which was in this instance the long Spanish romance in prose, called the Diana of Jorge de Montemayor.

Shakespeare's classically influenced early comedy was The Comedy of Errors (c. 1589-94). In this play, he resorted towards

Plautus' farcical play The Menaechmi (Twins). The story about two twins (Antipholus) seeking to locate his brother who has disappeared, and being joined by a clever servant (Dromio) who's twin is also missing, leads to an absurdity of false identity that is also meticulously checking the identity of its characters and self-knowing. The women in the play, including one who is the partner of Antipholus from Ephesus (Adriana) as well as the other, her sister (Luciana) are involved in an extensive discussion of issues about the wife's obedience and independence. Marriage can solve this issue at the conclusion which is often common in Shakespearean romantic comedy, however it's not after the plot's issues are a test for the characters' need to be aware of who they are as well as the things that men and women are expected to get from their relationship.

The earliest romantic comedy of Shakespeare is principally due to John Lyly is Love's Labour's Lost (c. 1588- the year 97) A sweet romp in the never-ending place of Navarre where the King as well as his comrades are taken away with the princess of France and her lady-in-waiting, to discuss a diplomatic issue which quickly turns into a contest of courtship. Much like in Shakespearean romantic comedies The girls decide that they are who they say they are and the person they're planning to marry; it isn't certain they will ever fall relationship, because they begin with a clear understanding of what they'd like to do. Boys however are prone to falling over with their absurdly pointless attempts to avoid romance for more serious interests. They make themselves look foolish, get embarrassed and ridiculed but are eventually forgiven their mistakes by females. Shakespeare wonderfully portrays the displeasure of males and self-assurance of females as his characters explore the dangerous yet enticing romantic world, as the verbal gymnastics that are part of the play show the awe as well as the delicious absurdity of getting in with love.

in "The Taming of the Shrew" (c. 1590 -(c. 1590-94), Shakespeare uses a technique of outlining which is likely to become an essential element in his romantic comedy productions. The plot of one is taken from Ludovico Ariosto's"I Suppositi" (Supposes that it was been transliterated to English in the hands of George Gascoigne), a girl (Bianca) goes on a shady affair with a guy who appears to be a tutor at the expense of her father who is determined to get her married to a wealthy suitor who is of his own choosing. The incorrect identities eventually get corrected, revealing the presumed tutor to be Lucentio wealthy and appropriate enough. In a single moment Bianca's smart sister Kate is a menace to (and terrorizes) the guys. Bianca's suitors have hired the brave Petruchio to hunt down Kate to ensure it is possible that Bianca who is the younger sister, can be able to get married. The plot of taming the wife is built on a ballad and folktale practice where men secure their dominance in the marital relation by beating their wives into submission. Shakespeare transforms this straightforward material, which is antifeminist, to a study of the battle to win supremacy in the marital relationship. In addition, even though he may decide in the play to favor masculine accomplishment over women however, he gives Kate the wit which allows her to understand how she could make the most of the benefit of herself. Kate is perhaps satisfied at the end of the day in a marriage built on humor and affection, even though Bianca, her sister Bianca is deemed to be spoilt.

The Early Legacies of William Shakespeare

In Shakespeare's explorations into English culture, including his romantic comedy, he placed his own stamp on a particular category, and made it his. It was also unusual. There was no formal definition for an English drama of history, and there was no visible rules for its development. The older Classical world recognized two broad classifications for category - tragedies and comedies. (This accounts is not inclusive of more specific categories, such as the satyr's plays.) Aristotle as well as other critics which includes but not only Horace have developed throughout the centuries, Classical meanings. Disaster dealt with the lives of disaster-stricken of famous people, and it was composed in verse raised with the intention of the setting an ancient mythological the world of gods and heroes: Agamemnon, Theseus, Oedipus, Medea, and others. Fear and pity are the most prominent psychological responses when the play tried to grasp, even if not entirely, the desires of gods supreme. Classical comedy however was a dramatization of the daily. The principal characters of the show were citizens from Athens and Romesuch as homeowners courtesans and servants, people who were rascals and such. Humour was quick contemporary, current, and relevant The lampooning was humorous or even violent. Participants were encouraged to examine the resemblances to their own lives, and also to laugh of recklessness and greed.

The English historical play did not have any kind of ideal theoretical framework. It was a creation of the ego which was a remarkable interpretation of present-day English historical events. It could be awry or humorous, or generally, an amalgam. Polonius's list of generic possibilities catches the ridiculous potential for unlimited hybridizations: "tragedy, comedy, history, pastoral, pastoral-comical, historical-pastoral, tragical-historical, tragical-comical-historical-pastoral," and so on (Hamlet, Act II, scene 2, lines 397-- 399). (By "pastoral," Polonius is most likely referring to a play that is based on love stories of the lives of rural shepherds and the corruptions that plagued city life or court.) Shakespeare's plays on history proved so successful during the fifteen90s' London theater that the editors of the complete Shakespeare plays, in 1623 decided to group his huge work under 3 categories which included comedy, historical and tragic plays. This category was created by the huge force due to its captivating popularity.

Shakespeare at the time of 1590 or later was the only real prototype for his English historical play: an obscure and huge drama titled The Famous Victories of Henry the Fifth (1583-- - 88) which told the story of Henry IV's infant son Prince Hal who was born in 1583, through the time of his teenage rebellion to his triumph over French in the Fight of Agincourt in 1415simply this was the basis for the material Shakespeare would later employ when writing three major productions, Henry IV, Part 1. Henry IV, Part 2 and Henry V. Shakespeare chose to not begin with the Prince Hal but rather with a more contemporary time in the history of Henry V's son Henry VI, and the civil wars which saw the dethronement of Henry VI by Edward IV, and then the rise to power at the time of 1483 by Richard III. This play proved extremely rich in themes and crucial disputes that he wrote four plays based on it. which was a "tetralogy" extending from Henry VI with 3 distinct segments (c. 1589 - 1589--93) up to Richard III (c. 1592-1592 - 94).

They were immediately effective. Recent reports suggest that the audience from the first 1590s were attracted in the tale (in Henry VI, Part 1) of the courageous Lord Talbot fighting in France against Witch Joan of Arc and her love interest and the French Dauphin and being weak in his brave efforts by the effeminacy of corruption within the household. Henry VI himself is, according to the way Shakespeare portrays him, an unfit king who was elevated to kinghood after the death of his father. He was also incapable to control the factions in his court and depressed personally due to his love for the sexy Frenchwoman, Margaret of Anjou. Henry VI is cuckolded by his lover and partner and The Duke of Suffolk and (in Henry VI, Part 2) is shown to be unable to defend his noble uncle and Duke of Gloucester in the face of opportunistic enemies. This leads to civil unrest as well as a rebellion of the lower classes (led by Jack Cade), and eventually a full-blown civil war in both the Lancastrian faction, supposedly led by Henry VI as well as the Yorkist plaintiffs who were under the direction by Edward IV and his brothers. Richard III completes the story by describing the tragic rising from Richard of Gloucester by the execution of his brother, the Duke of Clarence as well as Edward IV's two sons whom Richard was also a nephew. The totalitarian reign of Richard III eventually and without doubt to the newest and most successful heir to the throne, Henry Tudor, earl of Richmond. This is the person who is Henry VII, scion of the Tudor family and grandfather of queen Elizabeth I, who ruled between 1558 and 1603 as a result, all through the first decade and much more of Shakespeare's successful job.

The Shakespearean English historical play described the country's past in a period when the English nation was struggling with its own country identity, and was experiencing a fresh perception of authority. The Queen Elizabeth was able to bring peace and stability as well as a sense of freedom of war during her long years of reign. Her reign had thwarted from the Roman Catholic powers of the Continent and, in particular Philip II of Spain, and with the assistance of a hurricane at sea and a storm at sea, she had defeated Philip's plans to invade her kingdom through the epic Spanish Armada of 1588. In England the triumph of the nation was viewed as a divine deliverance. The second volume of Holinshed's Chronicles could be considered an important source for Shakespeare's earliest playwriting. The edition also was a celebration of the establishment to England as a leading Protestant nation, headed by an eminent and savvy queen.

Looking at the 1590s, history of the 15th century was seen as crucial in the recent past. England was coming out of an awful civil war that began that ended in 1485 with Henry Tudor's victory in defeating Richard III at the Fight of Bosworth Field. The principal characters in these conflicts, referred to as"the Wars of the Roses- including Henry Tudor, Richard III and the Duke of Buckingham, Hastings, Rivers, Gray, and a many more are well-known to contemporary English people.

The plays that were written by Shakespeare during the 1590s were centered to tell the story of a nation's emergence and their strong tendancy to distinguish between the heroes and villains. Shakespeare writes plays and not textbooks And he is not afraid to change dates, facts and the focus. Lord Talbot of Henry VI, Part 1 is a hero since the character dies to defend English interests from the fraudulent French. It is in Henry VI, Part 2 Humphrey the Duke of Gloucester who is degraded to the level of opportunists because he is in the best interest of the people and the nation as a whole. In the majority of cases, Richard of Gloucester is made to appear as an evil character, exemplifying one of the most vile aspects that a chaotic century brings about conflict between the civil and military. He is the source of strife, deceit and commits murder, as well as makes extravagant promises that he does not have any intention of retaining. It's a spectacular character simply because he's ingenious and inventive, but it's also a very dangerous threat. Shakespeare has every flaw the well-known custom depicts such as a hunchback, unbalanced glittering eye, and the shrewd genius of conspiracy. The truth is that Richard was not a evil person, according to the evidence to be the case that at least the murders he committed because of his political connections aren't much more gruesome than the shrewd elimination of any opposition from his successor, the legendary Henry VII. There is a difference in it was Henry VII lived to commission historians to write the story the way he wanted, but Richard was a victim of every single thing by defeat. The founder of the Tudor family and the grandpa of the Queen Elizabeth, Henry VII could have a reputation that Shakespeare had to honor as well. The Henry Tudor that he represents towards the end of Richard III is a God-fearing patriotic patriot, and a loving husband to the Yorkist princess that will inspire the future generation of Tudor Kings.

Richard III is a significant production, both in terms of the length of its run and also in the spectacular portrayal of its main role. It's referred to as a tragic piece in its name page, just like some of the earlier English historical plays. They surely present us with brutal deaths, and explain the fall of powerful men who were in high positions in order to suffer and wreak havoc. However, these aren't dramatic productions within the Classical meaning of the word.

They're composed of much more, and they close on a key important point: the emergence to the throne of the Tudor family that gives England an era of greatness under Elizabeth.

The story is a tale of pain and salvation, of a triumph from the great historical forces and incredible oversight, which will not allow England to endure the pain after she's returned to her original path of duty and courtesy. In this sense The early plays in the history genre have the same characteristics as love tragedies.

Chapter 4: The Middle Years Plays

Romantic Comedies

In the second quarter of 1590, Shakespeare was the first to excel in the romantic comedy genre that he was able to create. A Midsummer Night's Dream (c. 1595- 1696) is one among the best of his plays depicts the kind of outline techniques he used throughout The Taming of the Shrew and in other comedy works.

The main plot is about the Duke Theseus who is from Athens and his impending wedding to the Amazonian warrior Hippolyta who Theseus had just recently defeated and who has been admonished by Athens of his future bride. Their wedding is the end of the story. The couple share the final event along with the four lovers, Hermia as well Lysander, Helena and Demetrius leaving in the woods close by in order to break the Athenian law, and then fight one another and then go through several tangled up situations. In the end, all gets righted through fairy-like magic, even though they aren't less than a bit agitated. Oberon is the king of fairies, argues with his queen Titania about a shrewd boy and punishes her for it by making her to drop for the crime of an Athenian craftsman who wears the head of an assassin. They are on the trail to prepare a scene in preparation for the marriage that is scheduled to take place between Theseus with Hippolyta. Therefore, 4 distinct plots or hairs are connected to the other. Even with the shortness of the story, it is a masterpiece built by an artist and constructed.

A variety of stories encourages different ways of how love is experienced. For two human couples, falling for the love of their lives is a risk and the long-lasting friendship of the two women is threatened and ruined due to the rivalries of heterosexual love. A final shift towards heterosexual relationships appears to be a result that was a dream, and certainly a pain, after where they emerge amazingly back to their former versions of themselves. The marital conflict between Oberon as well as Titania is more alarmingly an affair in which women are embarrassed until she bows to the demands of her spouse. Similar to Hippolyta is a Amazon warrior queen who had to bow her will to that of her lover. Parents and daughters are not happier until they dream that, like the whole thing is sorted out with the help that is Puck or Oberon. It is as it is a relationship that lasts for a long time and a fight for excellence where the man has the advantage.

The Merchant of Venice (c. 1596- 97) utilizes a double plot structure that allows for a contrast between a story of romance with one that is at the edge of tragic. Portia is a perfect illustration of a romantic heroine in the mature Shakespeare comedy works She is funny, rich and demanding in her expectations of the way she wants men to behave and adept at wrapping her self in male disguise to make her presence visible. Portia is committed to the will of her father but is determined to ensure to get Bassanio. She slays the tangled legal issues of Venice even though the other guys have failed. Shylock is the Jewish loan holder, is on the point of requesting an ounce of meat from Bassanio's great buddy Antonio to pay to repay a loan.

Portia is a hindrance to the process in a manner that is smart as well as the shyster. In the play, compassion gets shakily stabilized. Shakespeare's portrayal of Shylock as a character who's in a state of distress by his Christian adversaries and ready to require the aid of an eye, according to the old law. Then Portia successes, not only not only with Shylock at the law court and in her wedding to Bassanio.

Much Ado About Absolutely nothing (c. 1598- 99) explores the subject of power and has a difficult to court, and again in an revealingly dual story. The heroine, a young woman from the classic story, which that is an adaptation of Italianate fiction, is captivated by an aristocratic young man named Claudio who has succeeded in winning his attention and is now considering it his duty of pleasure to get a wife. Claudio is so ignorant of Hero (as her name is) and he is gullibly relying on the fake proof provided by the antagonist of the tale, Don John, that she's been in love with numerous people which includes an evening on the day of the wanted wedding. The other guys, as well, which includes Claudio's superior officer Don Pedro, and Hero's father, Leonato, are all ready to believe the lies of Don John. Funny situations save Hero from being a victim of her accusers, and show the men that they're fools. In the meantime, her cousin, Beatrice, finds it difficult to shake off her suspicions regarding men, even though she is enthralled by Benedick and is skeptical of the idea of marriage. The barriers for romantic understanding are internal as well as mental, and can be overcome by the jovial sharing of their best acquaintances, who recognize the fact that Beatrice and Benedick have been made to be to be together by their honesty and wit If they could only overcome their fears of being out-witted by one another. It could be described as an amazing rewrite to The Taming of the Shrew The amusing battle between two sexes can be equally engaging and complicated, however it is the only way to find something more akin to respect and equal rights for both genders.

Rosalind In As You Like It (c. 1598- 1600) uses the now well-known technique of camouflage when she is the boy tries to achieve the goals of encouraging an important and wealthy sexual relationship between the two sexes. Like in the other productions, Rosalind is more mentally stable in her maturity and maturity than the son, Orlando. Orlando does not possess a formal training and has rough, but is essentially nice and attractive. The child of the Duke who is banned and is forced, and in turn, to go in trouble with her beloved close friend Celia as well as the court fool, Example. While Rosalind's masculine camouflage appears initially intended to aid in being able to get through an unfriendly woodland, it soon serves an even more fascinating purpose. In the role of "Ganymede," Rosalind befriends Orlando by offering him a treatment in the realm of romance. Orlando is in desperate need for such help, happily takes it on and keeps enchanting with his "Rosalind" (" Ganymede" acting as her self) as if she was certainly an actual woman. Her humorous and humorous observations about the irresponsibility of puppy love edify Orlando's over-inflated and unpractical "Petrarchan" position as the young love-struck lover who writes poetry for his partner and then sticks them on the trees. When he realizes that love isn't just a fantasy that is based on a set of preconceived notions, Orlando is all set to become the partner of the real woman (actually an untrained boy clearly) that is presented to him in a new Ganymede-Rosalind. Others in the show further understand the amazing absurdity of love by their differing perspectives: Silvius, the pale-faced lover who is driven by pastoral love; Phoebe, the disdainful love interest he idolizes William and the country bumpkin and Audrey the wench of the nation as well as, observing and discussing every possible form of recklessness in human behavior, the clown Example and the unruly tourist Jaques.

Twelfth night (c. 1600- 02) explores the same concept that is female camouflage. Viola is a victim of Illyria after a boatwreck, and then required to dress in the form of a man to be able to join the

Duke's court Orsino and falls in love with the Duke and utilizes the camouflage to excuse for an academic procedure similar to the one provided to Rosalind in Orlando. Orsino is as incongruous an amour as you could think of; he is a pathetic courtroom keeper to the Lady Countess Olivia and is satisfied with the pathetic romance melancholy that the duke writhes. In reality, Viola is "Cesario," has the capacity to stir inside him a true desire for love and friendship. They become friends forever and then competing for the affections of Olivia until the presto shift in Shakespeare's stage magic. It has the capacity to recreate "Cesario" to her woman's clothes and thus presents to Orsino the flesh-and-blood lady had only considered. A shift from friendship with a partner to heterosexual unions is constant in Shakespearean comedy. The woman is the self-aware and constant, loyal one and the male must be able to learn from his female counterpart. Similar to the other productions too, Twelfth Night nicely plays the courtship theme in an additional plot that centers around Malvolio's self-deception about being wanted by Olivia-- an illusion which can be reacted to solely through the satirical tools of embarrassment and direct exposure.

The Merry Spouses of Windsor (c. 1597-1601) is an intriguing divergence in comparison to the standard Shakespearean romantic comedy because it's not set in a distant location such as Illyria or Belmont or even the forests of Athens instead, but located in Windsor which is a robustly wealthy town close to Windsor Castle situated in the center of England. It is not clear if the custom was that the Queen Elizabeth would have liked to see Falstaff as a romantic couple. The play has a little that is romance (the tale that follows Anne Page and her suitor Fenton is a bit lost amid numerous other happenings) However, the play's portrayal of women especially of two "merry partners," Girlfriend Alice Ford and Girlfriend Margaret Page it reveals what's often the case with women depicted in these dramas: they're lovely committed, faithful and chaste, as well as charmingly self-possessed. Falstaff is a fitting smack for their brilliance, becomes an scapegoat character who must be publicly shamed to shed towards him the flaws of human nature which Windsor civilization is determined to eliminate.

Completion of the Histories

In the course of writing the exquisite romantic comedy plays, Shakespeare also brought to the end (for at least a while) at a minimum) his writing project fifteenth century English history. He completed 1589and 94, he wrote the Tetralogy of Henry VI Edward IV, as well as Richard III and Richard III, Shakespeare brought the plot to 1485 then, in 1594--96 an epic play on John who focuses on a specific time period (the thirteenth century) that set it distinct from his previous history productions, Shakespeare moved to the 14th and 15th centuries as well as the story of Richard II, Henry IV, and Henry's famous infant son Henry V. That inversion of historical order in the two tetralogies helped Shakespeare to conclude his epic sweep of the late middle ages English history by introducing Henry V, a hero and king which Richard III would never claim to be.

Richard II (c. 1595-1595 - 96) which was written in verse that is blank, a dark play on politics in a deadlock. The text is devoid of comedy, aside from the witty scene that the new King, Henry IV, should adjudicate the competing assertions of the Duke York and the Duchess of York who first want to see his son Aumerle punished for treason while the second one, who appeals to mercy. Henry is able to offer mercy on this particular occasion because he's been crowned king, and thus gives this situation a positive move. However, earlier, the mental state was bleak. Richard is a king who was brought up from an early age to the title of King, displays recklessness in his role as a king. He slams his first cousin Henry Bolingbroke (later to become Henry IV) although the king appears to be responsible for ordaining the death of an uncle. If Richard holds the dukedom Lancaster from Bolingbroke in the absence of legally-authorized authority, he's in a position to eject several nobles as well as to force Bolingbroke's return to exile. The return of Bolingbroke, as well, is illegal, however it's a fact as well. When a large number of nobles (consisting of York) are on Bolingbroke's cause, Richard is forced to give up. What is right and wrong in this battle for power are in doubt. It is an unreliable source of information, without a sense of ethics required. Henry IV is an incredibly than capable leader, however his legitimacy is damaged due to his crimes (including the apparent acceptance of Richard's execution Richard) as well as his rebellion seems to be a way to encourage the barons oppose him. Henry eventually dies unsatisfied.

The king who died Henry IV will hand his control of the royal court to the young Hal or Henry or, more recently Henry V. It's a disappointing prospect for both the deceased monarch and also to guests of his court because prince Hal has been distinguished in the past mainly due to his love of hanging out with a dishonest and engaging Falstaff. Hal's attempts to reconcile with dad are rewarded for the moment and especially so in the event that Hal helps save his father's life during the Battle in Shrewsbury however (specifically during Henry IV, Part 2) his record as a istrel will not let him go. Everyone suffers from the sway of his recklessness as well as Falstaff as the most prominent figure. For these reasons, the king's son should publicly denounce his previous comrade in the bars and on the highway. But much of the repudiation can rip from his soul and viewers. Falstaff with all his booze and recklessness can be a joy to watch and charming. He represents the character of Hal the spirit of a younger energy that is only left with the greatest of regret when the young man assumes his to become a man and assumes the title as crown prince. Hal does all the above with ease and then goes through to defeat the French well in The Fight of Agincourt. His high-energy jigs can be element that draws people to Hal. The ages and the position have an enormous personal price: Hal ends up being not as frail and more a symbol of an eminent the power of.

In his plays from the 1590s The young Shakespeare was focusing to a high stage on romantic comedy as well as English historical plays. These two categories are each other: one deals with the courtship process and marriage and marriage, whereas the second examines the career of a boy growing into a worthy King. At the very end of the plays dealing with history is Henry V have any sort or romantic connection with women, and this particular example stands unlike courtships that are found in the romantic comedy shows: Hal is given the princess of France to be his reward, as a reward for being a tough and strong man. Hal takes on the role of lead in the sweet scene where he invites his bride to be part of an official marriage. In romantic comedy plays as well as English dramas about history the boy is able to carry through the potentially dangerous but rewarding paths to social and sexual maturity.

Romeo and Juliet

Other than the early Titus Andronicus, the only additional play Shakespeare composed prior to 1599 and is considered tragic includes Romeo and Juliet (c. 1594- 1996) It's quite unusual of the tragedy plays which are set to be written. It was written more or less around the time Shakespeare was composing A Midsummer Night's Dream, Romeo and Juliet is a good example characteristics of romantic comedy. Romeo and Juliet don't have the same status or social standing such as Hamlet, Othello, King Lear as well as Macbeth. They're the boys and girl who live next to each other, captivating not because of their philosophical views, but due to their romantic love for one their partner. They're character types that suitable for Classical comedy because they aren't from the upper classes. Their wealthy families are essentially socially privileged. The energy with which Capulet and his wife seek to the Count of Paris to be their son-in law is a sign of their ambition to develop their social status.

In this way, the opening half of Romeo and Juliet is hilarious, while the enjoy verse style recalls A Midsummer Night's Dream. The absurdity of Mercutio as well as the Nurse fits perfectly with the comical humour of the initial scenes. Romeo who is engaged to Rosaline who we will never encounter, is a comic character like Silvius from As You Like It. The self-aware and adventurous Juliet shares a similarity to protagonists in romantic comedy. Juliet has the capacity to guide Romeo regarding the manner of being unaffected and open about their feelings instead of the tear-strewn vocals of the wooer from Petrarchon.

The story is ultimately an incredibly tragic piece of work, as is expected and definitely warns the audiences at the very beginning that the lovers have been "star-crossed." However, the vision of tragedy does not resemble that or that of Hamlet and King Lear. Romeo as well as Juliet are normal, decent young people who are sucked into a myriad of circumstances that are outside their own lives: the animosity between their two families, the misunderstandings that prevent Juliet from being able to inform her parents who she's married, or even the tragic coincidences (such as the erroneous interpretation of the letter addressed to Romeo to warn him about the Friar's plan to prepare Juliet for recuperation from a sleep-like death). But there's also the element of personal accountability on which the majority of mature tragedies are based in the event that Romeo decides to take revenge for the demise of Mercutio by murdering Tybalt and is aware that doing this act will scupper the gentle beauty of forbearance which Juliet is a model for him to follow. Romeo recognizes the male social pressures of his male companions which leads to tragedy. some degree from his decision. But there is so much involved that the reader ultimately sees Romeo as well Juliet as a love-themed tragedywhich celebrates the beautiful innocence of puppy love as well as expressing regret for a world that is not caring and triggering a psychological response that is different from the one generated by others tragic dramas. Romeo and Juliet will be, finally, "Poor sacrifices of our enmity" (Act V Scene 3, Line 334). The emotional reaction that it triggers is strong however it's not like the one evoked in tragic play after 1599.

The "Problem" Plays

Whatever was the motivation, between 1599to 1599-- Shakespeare was able to turn with uncompromising strength toward the exploration of dark questions like vengeance and sexual jealousy, aging, middle-age crisis and finally dying. Perhaps he realized the way in which his life was advancing to a different stage, one that was more complicated and difficult events. Perhaps he believed that he had a sense that he'd gotten the historical and romantic comedy plays and the psychological paths of maturity that they offered. Whatever the reason He began writing not just his greatest tragedy plays but a variety of plays that are difficult to define in a the category. In some instances, they are classified in the form of "issue" plays or "issue" comedy plays. A thorough analysis of the plays are essential for understanding this time transition from 1599 through 1605.

The 3 issues of plays to this time are All's Well that is Over Well, Measure for Measure as well as Troilus as well as Cressida. All's Well is a funny conclusion that ends with marriage approval however, it does so in a manner that raises tough moral questions. The fact that Count Bertram cannot at first be happy with the marriage proposal of Helena who is a lady of low social status who been raised in his prestigious family and who has gotten Bertram as her spouse through her apparent awe-inspiring solution to the French King. Bertram's reluctance to accept the obligations of marriage worse when he reveals his romantic desires towards an Florentine lady, Diana, whom he is looking to romance without marriage. Helena's strategy to resolve this problem is to use the bed technique. She replaces herself with Bertram's bed to take advantage of an assigned assignment, and then after the incident, she calls her difficult lover to answer for her actions for being pregnant with their baby. The goal is achieved through an ethically ambiguous method that marriage can be seen as an unwise organization upon the assumption of security of the romantic comedy. Finding closure and maturity in the psychological realm is not easy; Helena is more uncertain hero as Rosalind as well as Viola.

Measure for Measure (c. 1603- 04) also employs the bed method, and serves the same purpose, although it is used in more ambiguous situations. Isabella who is on the verge of becoming a nun finds out that she's attracted the sexual inclination of Lord Angelo who is the vice-ruler of Vienna working in the odd absence that is the Duchess. Isabella's plea to Angelo to save her brother's life and that of her brother (Claudio) was ordered to fornicate with his wife, is answered by a demand for her to spend time with Angelo or renounce Claudio's existence. The moral dilemma is solved using an elaborate scheme (created by Duke disguised) to replace Isabella the woman (Mariana) with whom Angelo was to marry but who refused because she was unable to make an wedding dowry. The Duke's motivations behind the replacements and a sloppy appearance remain a mystery, although maybe his goal is to find out what diverse characters in the play can do when confronted with a variety of choices that seem improbable. Angelo is revealed as an ethically flawed man an aspiring killer and seducer but who's ultimately content to be disqualified from his illegal activities. Claudio discovers that he's a coward enough to want to die by any means which includes the physical and psychological intimidation of his sister and Isabella realizes that she has the ability to feel bitterness and resentment, even though the most important thing is that she realizes the ability to accept her rival's forgiveness. The kindness of her, as well as the Duke's strategies, allow to end reconciliation and forgiveness, however during the process, the character and significance of marriage are severely examined.

Troilus as well as Cressida (c. 160102) is among the most speculated and confused of the 3 works. As a matter of categorization the play is essentially not classifiable. The story isn't even remotely hilarious, especially when it concludes like it did in the tragic deaths of Patroclus and Hector and the impending loss by the Trojans. The ending isn't even considered to be normal when it comes to romantic comedy. In the play, two lovebirds, Troilus and Cressida, become separated from one to the point of anger and discontent over the loss of their love. This is a staged historical piece in the sense that it is which concludes with the epic Trojan War celebrated in Homer's Iliad but the purpose of the play isn't just to tell the tale of war. It is a tragedy in the sense that it's a bit puzzling the fact that the main characters of the drama (apart the character of Hector) do not die in the final scene as the overall mental state is that of despair and anger instead of a terrifying anger. The play could be viewed as a satire, and the sad comments that are made by Thersites and Pandarus provide an oblique observation on the interconnectedness between the war and sexual lust. The play was, in a manner of speaking, ambiguous. drama was placed in the

Folio 1623 in among the history and tragic works, creating an entirely separate classification. In these dramas Shakespeare began to open up to himself an array of brand new questions in relation to category and sexuality of the human.

The play was written in 1599 (the identical year of Henry V.) or in 1600, likely in the time of opening the World Theatre on the south river Thames, Julius Caesar shows as well the evolution of Shakespeare's plays towards dark themes and tragic. Also, it is an historical play in the broadest way, dealing with the non-Christian world of 16 centuries prior to the time that Shakespeare composed his works. Roman historical events opened up to Shakespeare an era in which the purpose of his plays could not be immediately identified. (Click on this link to watch the video of Caesar's most famous speech.) The characters from Julius Caesar otherwise translate the epic incident of the assassination Caesar as a situation in which gods are angry or uninterested or simply aren't there. A wise Cicero says, "Men might interpret things after their style, / Clean from the purpose of the important things themselves" (Act I Scene 3 lines 34 35).

Humanity's history as seen through Julius Caesar appears to follow the same pattern, but with a pattern that is recurring rather than divinely ordained. Caesar is content with his moments of achievement, but he's ultimately beaten to a stalemate by conspirators. Brutus and Cassius succeed in gaining control, but they don't last lengthy. The efforts of Brutus to protect Roman republicanism as well as the flexibility that the citizens of Rome had to rule themselves according to Senate customs end at the expense of his very liberties loved the most. The two of them Cassius are destined to die during the Fight of Philippi. The two characters are absolutely terrible and especially Brutus because their characters' essentials are fates; Brutus is a pretty decent man, but also proud and determined, and those characteristics eventually result in the death of his character. Shakespeare's very first important drama is Roman in spirit as well as Classical in the concept of the villainous characters. It demonstrates how Shakespeare required to know from Classical examples as he went about looking for models that could be used for tragedy.

The Tragedies

Hamlet (c. 1599 1601) On his part, opts for the most horrific model, which is closer to the one in Titus Andronicus and

Kyd's The Spanish Catastrophe. The way it is written, Hamlet is a tragedy of vengeance. It has characteristics that can be that are found in Titus as well: a leading actor who has the burden to avenge a sly criminal action against the protagonist's family, a clever villain as well as the appearance that of the spirit of the murdered person, the appearance of mental illness to dispel any suspicions about the criminal and the role of the play, as a way to evaluate the villain as well as many more.

But to explore these contradictions will help to identify what's amazing in Hamlet because it isn't able to be just a vengeance tragedy. The character of Hamlet is distinctive within the realm of ethical dilemmas, but most especially in his discovering a method of executing his terror command, without appearing to be the cold-blooded murderer. Hamlet can be bloody particularly when he murders Polonius believing that the old man buried within Gertrude's rooms is the King Hamlet is commissioned to murder. This act seems authentic and well-thought out however Hamlet recognizes at the exact the fact that he's made a mistake. The untrue man, even if Polonius is responsible for the murder himself by his constant surveillance. Hamlet recognizes that he's created a mess in paradise and has to be punished for his actions. As the play comes to an close, Hamlet experiences his fate during a fight with Polonius's son, Laertes, Hamlet analyzes his personal story and sees it in the light of what Providence has made important. Through putting himself into the writ of Providence and firmly believing in the fact that "There's a divinity that forms our ends, / Rough-hew them how we will" (Act V Scene 2, lines 10-11), Hamlet finds himself in the position of being ready for a fate would have been his dream. Hamlet also discovers a possibility to murder Claudius almost in a moment of spontaneity, without premeditation in repulse for what Claudius did to him.

Hamlet so finds no significance in his own tale. Additionally Hamlet has sought significance in every kind: his mother's hasty marriage, her weak-willed taking the will of her father as well as her brother, the fact that he was observed by his previous great friends Rosencrantz and Guildenstern as well as many more. The words he speaks of are often depressing as well as non-stop honest and philosophically profound, in his exploration of the origins of memories, friendships and romantic bonding and filial love. He also considers sensual infliction, destructive behaviors (drinking and sexual desires) in general, as well as each phase of the human experience.

The most remarkable thing about Shakespeare's epic tragic plays (Hamlet, Othello, King Lear, Macbeth, and Antony and Cleopatra many of the most famous of them) is the fact that they go with such an enthralling series of human experiences particularly the emotions which are typical of the maturing years of the human life cycle. The Hamlet character is 30 years old and one discoversthat at this age, one is likely to think as if the world appears to be "an unweeded garden/ That grows to seed. Things rank and gross in nature/ Have it solely" (Act I scene 2 lines 135-and 135-137). Shakespeare was a young man of 36 when he wrote the comedy. Othello (c. 1603 -2004) explores the issue of sexual jealousy in marriage relationships. King Lear (c. 1605- 06) revolves around the aging process, generational disputes and feelings of resentment. Macbeth (c. 1606 -07) is a saga of aspiration that's mad enough to drive out a father person who is standing in his way. Antony and Cleopatra wrote something in 1606to 07, in the period when Shakespeare was around 42 Research studies the fascinating and ultimately disconcerting phenomenon of midlife crises. Shakespeare takes his readers through the life of these characters and he struggles of capturing, in an awful way, their horrors and pitfalls.

The plays have a deep interest in family and household relationship. In Othello Desdemona, the sole daughter of Brabantio who is an old senator from Venice that dies in sorrow because his daughter got married to a dark-skinned man that is older than her by a few years, and who is from a different style of life. In Othello, Desdemona is quickly content, despite her obstinacy, until an odious sexual desire develops in him and without any reason, aside from his personal fears as well as his vulnerability to Iago's assertions that it's "natural" for Desdemona to seek out sexual pleasure in a man who is a part of her heritage. Instinctively unjustified fear and disdain for women, and somewhat distrustful of his masculinity, Iago will be able to alleviate his internal torture by convincing others as Othello the inevitable destiny of their lives will be a cuckolding. It is a tragedy in the sense that it is adroitly illustrating the traditional Classical concept of a powerful man who is afflicted with the hamartia or terrible defect in the sense that, in the scene where Othello is grieving, he's a man who "loved not sensibly, but too well" (Act V Scene 2, line 354). The play is worth recollecting, however it is true that Shakespeare did not have any ties to the Classical model. Hamlet is one example. It is a work that does not perform well when viewed when viewed in Aristotelian concepts. Looking for Aristotelian character called hamartia has lead all of the time to the standard claim that Hamlet suffers from melancholia as well as an insufficiency of action in a convincing version of the play argues that finding the correct approach is a huge problem both for him and everyone else. Hamlet has examples on both side of people whose honest acts result in fatal mistakes or bizarre contradictions (Laertes, Fortinbras), as well as his own impulsive execution of the man whom he believes to be Claudius locked in his mom's chambers turns out to be mistake for which the play's protagonist knows paradise is holding the blame.

Dads and children are in the middle of the main problem within King Lear. In this scenario, Shakespeare follows the same pattern he usually does in his later productions: he removes the married partner out of the story to ensure that the father as well as the daughter(s) will be left to deal with one another. (Compare Othello, The Winter season's Tale, Cymbeline, The Tempest as well as his own life in which his relationship to his child Susanna especially seem to have been more important for him than his divorced marriage to Anne.) Lear's exile from his favorite daughters, Cordelia, because of her insincere refusal to express his love as the core of her character and carries on the aging King the terrible burden of being snubbed and rejected by his angry daughters Goneril as well as Regan. The play's second plot the Earl of Gloucester commits a similar error by ignoring his sweet child Edgar who, in turn, puts himself to his computer-incompetent child Edmund. Both of these fathers who make a mistake will eventually be supported by their loyal children they've exiled and not long after the play is gone to its absolute limits the idea that evil is able to thrive in a hostile world.

Gods seem uninterested or perhaps absent completely; appeals to them for assistance are ignored while the torrent of riches pours over those who depend on traditional pieties. One of the reasons I love it in the play is it's portrayal of important characters who require them to look for answers to philosophical questions that will protect the heart from despair and apathy by constantly saying that the world owes us the least bit of respect. The peace of mind realized through Edgar and Cordelia are the ones that depend not on a god who is supposely existent, instead, but an inner moral force that demands one to remain honest and charitable because it is the case that life can be incredibly cruel and inhuman. The drama reveals the terrible expenses from those who are steadfast in their morality and truth, yet it provides readers, or the audience, with confidence that it's more desirable to be Cordelia rather than an Edmund or a Goneril or an Edgar rather than the Edmund. Edmund.

Macbeth is, in many ways the most horrifying of Shakespeare's plays, due to its scathing evaluation of the innermost being of an individual who's decent in all ways, however, his heart isn't strong enough to achieve power at any price. Macbeth is a sensitive poet, perhaps that understands the risks that go along the contemplated act of murder. Duncan is a godly King and his guest. It is a regicide, murder as well as an offense to hospitality's spiritual obligations. Macbeth recognizes Duncan's virtues are as angels do "trumpet-tongued," will plead against "the deep damnation of his taking-off" (Act I 7 scene 7 lines 1920). One thing in the other direction is a personal desire, something Macbeth realizes is an ethical lapse. Macbeth's question about why Macbeth is still committing murders partially answered by the dark threats that are a part of Macbeth's 3 Weird Sisters, who recognize Macbeth's sensitivity to their predictions, as well as the terrifying strength of his spouse who pushes him to the crime by labelling the unwillingness of his wife as unmanly. In the end, though, the accountability lies with Macbeth. Macbeth's egregious lack of moral integrity is a challenge to the audience, and possibly connects to it. Devotion and morality of characters like Macduff only barely compensate for what's horribly weak about the main character.

Antony and Cleopatra explore human vulnerability through terms that are not as emotionally frightening. The love story are definitely one of worldly failing. The Lives of Plutarch gave Shakespeare the concrete example of a courageous general who lost his reputation and self-esteem through his infatuation with a certain beautiful, yet dangerous lady. Shakespeare does not alter any of the scenarios: Antony dislikes himself for being with Cleopatra in Egypt with Cleopatra and agrees to marry to Octavius Caesar's sister Octavia to gain recovering his position as a member of the Roman set of three. He does not respect Octavia but ultimately losing the battle of Actium due to the ferocious attraction he has to Cleopatra and dies in Egypt as a beaten, old soldier. Shakespeare is able to create an entertaining portrayal of middle-age crisis. Antony is a bit agitated about the loss of his sexual power and his place in the society. His sexually ferocious life in Egypt is clearly an attempt to reclaim and confirm his diminished male strength.

However, it is true that the Roman model doesn't make Shakespeare's plays the undeniably moral decision that is made the case in Plutarch. The play Antony as well as Cleopatra Roman behavior does encourage respect for duty and success, but as shown in the character of young Octavius the character, it's also extremely male-dominated and demeaning of females. Octavius wants to capture Cleopatra and guiding her to triumph back to Romewhich is to confine the rowdy female and bring the woman under the control of males. In the event that Cleopatra is not convinced as a good thing, she decides to take a suicide, rather than being embarrassed from an male patriarchal. The suicide note of Cleopatra claims that she is been called "great Caesar ass/ Unpolicied" (Act V Scene 2, lines 30730- 308). It is a great choice to choose the quick-lived dream of that she had a successful relationship with Antony as well as Antony. Both were God-like and unbound, just as Isis and Osiris who are lauded as strong lovers even though the reality situations of their lives often were gruelling and absurd. The story is a deliberate shaky one, however when it is at its best, it inspires an image of human accomplishment that is far from the vile evil that ravages our souls like Macbeth and King Lear.

2 tragic late plays use the older Classical world as the setting however they do it in a way that is deeply depressing. Shakespeare seems to have been a lot preoccupied with human greed and apathy throughout the years. Timon from Athens (c. 1605 -8) Most likely, a sloppy play that was never produced initially, portrays a successful and famous man known for his generosity. After he discovers that he's exceeded his resources, he looks to the people he thought were his great friends for the kinds of help he's given but discovers they have no memory of them. In a state of utter isolation, Timon rails against all people and is unable to accept any kind relief, including that of a well-meaning friendship or compassion of a former service. He dies alone. The bitterness

that is unsatisfying in this story is only partially diluted through the tale of general of the army Alcibiades He has been the focus of Athenian regret and the loss of memory, but manages to restore his power at the conclusion. Alcibiades attempts to negotiate an concessions to the sad state of mankind; Timon will have none of it. Rarely has an unrelievedly dismayed play composed.

Coriolanus (c. 1608) Also, Coriolanus represents the pathetic responses of a city toward its hero from the army. It's a complicated issue due to the fact that Coriolanus is angered by his mother and the conservatives he has as allies plays a role in politics within Rome in which he's not well-suited. Some of his best friends suggest to repress his raunchy speeches until he's elected to the office, however Coriolanus's speech is plain enough to make a difference in this manner. His resentment for the plebeians, and their leaders and tribunes is uncompromising. The way he views his political ideology, although not a day without a snob is in fact is advanced.

The citizens are, the author claims not able to govern them in a sensible manner. But his anger just adds to the problem and leads to an exile, which leads him back to rule his home city in alliance with his former foe and dear friend Aufidius. If his mom is seen out in the city, to defend her cause and those of fellow Romans He resigns, and becomes defeated and is an incarnation of a mom's son and is unable to establish the self-confidence he has. In a tragic piece, Coriolanus is again bitter humorous, and ends with humiliation and defeat. This is a highly effective and powerful play that reveals the philosophical mindset of despair and bitterness which can be seen in the works of Shakespeare through the beginning in the 1660s.

Chapter 5: William Shakespeare

Mention the name William Shakespeare to students of English across the globe and you'll be met with a array of reactions that range from a defiant expression of total indifference to complete awe and horror. There will always be a couple who are genuinely thrilled by the idea of reading the Bard of Avon's entire work, however most of the time, Shakespeare is consigned to the list of most prestigious academic dreads, alongside Algebra, Pythagoras, the Corn Laws, Photosynthesis, Physics all in all, and poetry by Ezra Pound!

But this is not just an inference because the most common misconceptions regarding William Shakespeare are to say at the very least, unfounded leading to the genius of the world's most famous actor being ignored because of fear and ignorance.

When you're trying to understand any major literary figure it is important to be approached from three different points of view. The first is that you are able to access the writings of your author and the plays, novels or poetry printed on black-and-white paper, for you to experience and read your own.

Second, you need to place the writer's work within its historical an historical context by learning something about the community that your writer was a part of. That doesn't necessarily mean that you have to go through a detailed history course but, in fact What you really need is a quick snapshot of your author's lifestyle as well as the time. Dates and relevant events in a larger context can be helpful, however should you be able to find some of the biggest scandals and gossip of the moment and especially when the topic of your research was involved in the scandal, all the more.

In order to complete your sketch, to complete your picture, you should consider a look around the writer's lifestyle including warts and all and attempt to create an image of their personality in addition to the literary masterpieces they've written down on paper to be preserved for posterity, however, you can also draw inspiration from diaries personal letters and other items too.

However, with regards to William Shakespeare this fine theory is extremely difficult to apply due to a variety of reasons. The first and most important reason is that Shakespeare did not intend that any one could read his works; They were designed to be performed on stage. What you see on a page isn't the story that young William thought of in the first place. Line-by-line, he provided his actors with written scripts for each of the plays that were then performed before being discarded. It took seven years after the death of Shakespeare to get two of his actors to gather his plays and release the plays as"the "First Folio" of 1623. The goal to John Heminges and Henry Condell were in order to "keep the memory of so worthy a friend and fellow worker alive" but not like you would think that they were attempting to impose torture on the children of the in the future. Thus, starting from the very beginning be sure to see Shakespeare's works Shakespeare in action, whether it's live on television or on film, as it's the only method to fully understand what the writer was aiming for.

If you set Shakespeare's plays into context, you realise how far back that you're travelling. The queen Elizabeth I was seated on the throne in England throughout Shakespeare's lifetime, however Shakespeare was able to survive the final days of the Tudors as well as the emergence of the Stuart lineage, which culminated when James I. James I. Shakespeare's plays were popular with the royal household and monarchs as well as Shakespeare was certainly a major fame.

The story of the period is well-documented, but it is sad to say that the same cannot be said about William Shakespeare. If you are looking to dig into his personality, life and time, the reality of the situation is that there's very little tangible evidence.

AT THE age of 28, Shakespeare began to make appearances at London however, until 1564, his baptism was documented in 1564. He also recorded his wedding date was 1582 as well as the births of his children in 1583 as well as 85 and 1583, all of which took place within Stratford upon Avon. There is nothing else that Shakespeare has done throughout the first few years of his existence, exists and that's an excellent idea to build your confidence. Out of the countless books and biographies are available on shelves of books on Shakespeare regardless of the expert theories suggest for Shakespeare's early period, no one really knows the truth because there's not any evidence whatsoever for any of it.

Your OWN opinions about the young genius of Stratford upon Avon is as great as that of the other or women to be honest. Every day, anywhere around the globe, someone writes a book on Shakespeare So don't feel scared to formulate your own thoughts regarding the actor, begin with a fresh slate and investigate the world of Shakespeare with no preconceived notions. It will be awe-inspiring the things you'll find. Don't be astonished by the stoic, middle-aged, respectable and hairy Elizabethan Shakespeare wearing his iconic lace ruff. Instead, look up the young William as the crazy and wild country boy who was from Warwickshire that changed the face of literature in a positive way.

In THIS Journal, we'll take an in-depth look at three of Shakespeare's plays: Twelfth Night, Romeo and Juliet and Macbeth However, prior to beginning, we'll be practicing the principles we teach and then turn to the life of Shakespeare, as well as his society where Shakespeare lived to send our sights on the person behind the story.

To begin, and then from the beginning, you should go towards Stratford upon Avon, the center of the Shakespeare tourism business. Each and every building is associated with Shakespeare, at least the merchants claim but it will take some detective work to figure it all out.

The place where Shakespeare was believed to have been was born around 1900.

Shakespeare's birthplace, where he was believed to have been born at St. George's Day, 25th April 1564. There are two issues are that firstly, no one is able to confirm Shakespeare was born in this residence, even though there was a Shakespeare family's home at the day, and secondly there's no proof to support the time of birth. The baptismal records indicate that his birth date was during that time, but the circumstances might be too contemporary to be believed.

Shakespeare was supposedly dead on the 23rd of April, 1616. His tombstone at Holy Trinity Church, Stratford records, making it quite poetic for the numerous fans of Shakespeare were able to spin an excellent tale. Shortly after his death, the actor became a national institution. What could be more fitting than a famous Englishman coming into the world and departing at St George's Day, celebrated in honour of the patron saint of dragons of the entire nation of England. An ideal for a PR professional to come real!

Chapter 6: The Funerary Shakespeare Monument, Holy Trinity Church, Stratford

The majority of people have an notion of the fact that Mary Arden had something to be associated in the life of William Shakespeare, and she was actually his mother. If you go by the signs for tourists a short further away from Stratford towards the charming village of Wilmcote You can't miss Featherbed Lane and the 16th century, half-timbered home referred to all over the world in the name of Mary Arden's House. When she was married to John Shakespeare, the great bard's dad, it was believed to be Mary's home. However, recent research suggests some confusion with. The house next door "Glebe Farm" is far likely to be her house, though it is the Shakespeare Birth Place Trust cares for both homes and is worthy of a explore the area.

It's evident that no matter which home belonged to Mary's family, they were wealthy and well-known that the woman in that case was quite below her status as she teamed up with Shakespeare. Shakespeare.

The SHAKESPEARE'S were regarded as wild mob of rebubates. Although John was more successful than the majority of them as an accomplished Stratford manufacturer of gloves, he was not ever the Civic public figure he was to become. In 1552, he punished with a fine of a shilling, for creating the dung heap on the home of a neighbor on Henley Street. Elizabethan cities were quite revolting in regards to the disposal of sewage, however there were in place, and every road was a Muck Hill where people had to dispose of their feces, instead of the muck being left to decay in their backyard, or as in this instance, somewhere other's! It is interesting to note that locals always believed that if Shakespeare had a debt to you, it was a tough task to collect the money however, in this instance, John settled his fine promptly, and perhaps showed signs of earlier efforts to boost his reputation.

JOHN SHAKESPEARE JOHN SHAKESPEARE and Mary Arden are most likely to have got married in their wedding in the Parish Church of St. John the Baptist in Aston Cantlow, but there are no records that they were married in 1557 since Parish Records didn't come in the several years following this date. William was the 3rd child of John and Mary however, the two girls that preceded him died both during infanthood. It's up to you what your perspective obviously, it's good that William was able to survive since Bubonic plague ravaged Stratford at the age of 3 months old. But the likelihood is that his mother took him into the security of the home she shared with her family at Wilmcote till the worst threat had gone.

At the time William was in school His father was already a renowned figure in both business and social life and was on his path to becoming the Mayor of Stratford. Being an up-and-coming gentleman in the town, he took his sons, at the age of five old, to the King's New School, also called Stratford Grammar, and as we read within Shakespeare's "Seven Ages of Man" speech in As You Like It, maybe younger William was not a fan of his privilege much any time:

Every stage in the world with all of the players and women are just players.

There are exits for them and their entry points;

A man who in his moment of time is able to play many roles,

The acts of his are seven years old.

In the beginning, the baby

Pooping and mucus within the arms of a nurse.

And then, there was the grouchy student with the satchel,

and a sparkling face in the morning, moving like an octopus."

Indifferent to going to go to school.

It is a fact that it was a Tudor school day would run beginning at six in the morning to six in the evening, and included lessons that were based on only religious beliefs and classics. The masters were intolerant, beating students for even the tiniest mistake, and William was not too displeased as his father's business fell downhill, as this meant that he was removed from the school at the age of 13.

We're back in the realm of speculation regardless of how educated, as there is any evidence regarding William Shakespeare either entering or departing Stratford Grammar School. We'll find out later Shakespeare's reputation for being an un-educated ploughman would have him follow his path to London however it is likely that he did receive some basic schooling although he did so reluctantly as an Stratford youngster.

What transpired to youngsters? Will Shakespeare next really takes the biography writer into the realm of fantasy. Basically you can be just as accurate as any other. Most likely, he was working with his father to make gloves on Henley Street, but maybe the fact is that he wasn't at Stratford in the first place. Many believe that he sailed out to sea, and then sailed all over the world along with Sir Francis Drake on the "Golden Hind" as well as many other possibilities, some that were just as imaginative like the plots for Shakespeare's forthcoming play. However, whatever the fantasies that William had in his early years his reality, what faced him as an 18-year-old Stratford youngster in town led him into the ground with a huge hit.

If you've read the guides to tourist destinations You'll be able to take the journey of a romantic to Shottery and the stunning the shady cottage of Anne

Hathaway which is where William during his prime was courting.

However, there is a truth there is no way to get. Most likely as a result one roll of bales of hay Anne Hathaway claimed to have been sexy through William Shakespeare. This is a trap many a attractive youngster is caught in, prior to and after. Will was just eight years older, and it appears that marriage ensnaring had been the not-so-eligible female's motive. Anne's supporters made sure that Will was forced to make a decision in the matter. By May 1583 Will was married to an unmarried daughter named Susanna who was at the age of nineteen.

SHAKESPEARE was not a content young man. He was also financially limitations forced his family to relocate into the already overcrowded Henley Street house, where Will's children ranged in the ages of Edmund who was just two, Richard eight and Joan thirteen all the way to Gilbert 16. It's not a secret that Anne was no longer a fan of Shakespeare's sexual preferences in any form or way, but he was able to give birth to a pair of twins Hamnet as well as Judith in 1585. This added the burden of his obligations.

The future was awful to William Shakespeare, with no way out of the house at hand. Poaching excursions into Charlcote Park after Sir Thomas Lacy's deer were what life can be, however when Shakespeare was found guilty and dragged before a chief magistrate in charge the culprit was Sir Thomas himself. The evidence would show that Will had a very snarky actor who annoyed the unjust property owner beyond any measure, even writing a sexist and obscene song regarding Lacy the landowner, which Shakespeare displayed on the Charlotte Park gates for all to view.

From then on, the angry Sir Thomas was pursued by Will whenever he could to rob the young man of any pleasures from having a few hours of poaching.

Escaping was never an OPTION however, it was often served in the Stratford's Guild Hall, when visiting Theatre Companies would ply their business, and Shakespeare might have enjoyed an opportunity to see the performers in action. In light of the fact that Shakespeare has not been mentioned since the birth of the twins on 1585 and his first appearance in London 1592, we must try to rewrite certain details through some fun speculation. Perhaps Shakespeare was employed by an ensemble of actors that led him into London as a way to escape Sir Thomas Lacy and the wife and children back in Henley Street?

We know in 1587 that in 1587, the Queen's Men arrived to perform at Stratford one who was short after a brawl close to Oxford the scene of which one group had been killed by a knife to death. This is a guess however it could seem plausible to William Shakespeare to have stepped into the shoes of the dead man traveling towards London in absence of any basis, this would explain Shakespeare's complete disappearance from history books.

SHAKESPEARE'S reemergence as an London dramatist in 1592 was recorded by a fellow poet who was not all that complimentary. in his Groatsworth of Wit Bought with a Million of Repentance, the university-educated Richard Greene describes Shakespeare as "an upstart crow" who believes that "he is as well able to bombast out blank verse" like the rest of us.

Today, people are unable to accept that an uninformed Warwickshire youngster was in charge of creating the most dramatic work in literary work, which was the same throughout Shakespeare's life.

It's extremely difficult to pinpoint the dates of Shakespeare's plays. However, as of 1594, at least six of them were created, and he had purchased shares of the Lord Chamberlain's Men. Shakespeare continued to be a part of this theater company for the rest of his life that was later renamed modification to King's Men when Elizabeth I passed away and the king James succeeded to her.

The young country boy who was moving through the city of London was very prolific in his writing. However, it did not involve all work and no fun! When sexual frustration, coupled with a partner he couldn't endure and a wife he couldn't stand, were a regular an integral part of Stratford life, it is clear that he took advantage of the opportunities that could be found in America's capital. In many Shakespeare sonnets, you'll see an "dark-eyed beauty" who stole Shakespeare's heart. And despite the efforts of literary scholars throughout time the identity of her has not been discovered. There are also rumors the possibility that Shakespeare was bisexual and, on numerous occasion, doctors from that time were called to administer the infamous clap! the"clap!"

An amazing story is discovered in the diary of a barrister, who had a connection to Shakespeare and also his friend who was the famous actor Richard Burbage. A fervent Elizabethan lover was so enthralled by Burbage's portrayal as Richard III that she arranged for him to visit her for dinner that evening, however with the title "Richard III". Scallywag Shakespeare was enthralled by the plans being planned, showed up at the charming woman's home later than he had known was been planned.

The actor was admitted and while enjoying the luxuries of being famous, a warning was sent to him informing him that Richard III was at the entrance. While not even taking a breath Shakespeare answered by sending message that William the conqueror appeared to be ahead of Richard III, demonstrating his vast knowledge of the past and his clever interpretation.

How much MRS. SHAKESPEARE had a clue when she was in Stratford about her husband's carry off, is a mystery to us. however, the amount he paid home started to grow which suggests that maybe there weren't a lot of inquiries.

SHAKESPEARE returned back to Stratford in 1596. However, it was it was for tragic motives when his son Hamnet passed away. The reason for Hamnet's loss of life is unknown however it would mark the beginning of Shakespeare's male Shakespeare family and was extremely painful for the absent father.

WORD OF Shakespeare's acclaim in London was not yet reaching people in Stratford at the time, and then one year after the death of Hamnet and he ensured that anyone who looked over their shoulders at him was aware of how significant the man had grown to be. Shakespeare acquired "New Place", the largest and most luxurious house situated in Stratford however it is not on the tourism route. It is owned by the Birthplace Trust owns "Nash's House" which is a stunning all-black and white Tudor house that Shakespeare's daughter lived in along with her husband, lawyer Thomas Nash, but if you go to the gardens, you'll be on the spot that was "New Place".

The infamous destruction of New Place would have probably more been amused William Shakespeare, and the tale wouldn't have been appropriate in one of his most fanciful works. In the years following Shakespeare's death, a shrewd 18th Century vicar acquired New Place, which was famous as the Bard's Stratford residence. Like today, pilgrims came from all over the world to visit Shakespeare's home and the Reverend Gentleman was a bit irritated by this. The people would make him irritated more by requesting to view the Mulberry plant in the garden that was allegedly planted by Shakespeare himself. The vicar quickly put an end in the process by cutting the tree down!

When, later on, the local tax authorities decided to attempt to impose a rate charge on New Place they were dealt with a similar slack. The reverend gentleman promised that no official from the city could ever go over his limit to appraise the property which he did and destroyed New Place to prevent them from ever doing it! In one single crime of vandalism, the most vital part of America's Shakespearean history was destroyed.

However, during his time Shakespeare did not hesitate to undertake the demolition of a few properties that he had his own. This is how the world famous Globe Theatre came into being. Based on the popular Shakespeare plays that he chose to play The Lord Chamberlain's Men were a hugely successful financial institution and the landlord figured that they should also get some of the glory. After the lease of the theater expired in the year he demanded an enormous rent hike that Shakespeare and his colleagues were not a fan of. Through the years and years, the debates grew increasing in intensity until the irritated landlord made a threat to shut down the theater.

As was typical for that time, that land was the property of the owner of the land and he was in every right to take this action however, rather than make actors pay additional money, they were offered a brilliant plan. The Globe was part of Lord Chamberlain's Men. Lord Chamberlain's Men in terms of building materials. Therefore, in the dark of night, they demolished the plank of the theatre with planks and carried through into the River Thames. The current model of the Globe is situated almost at exactly the same spot as Shakespeare's 16th Century construction, but unfortunately burned down in a show in 1613.

The Great "WOODEN O" as Shakespeare often described the theatre he performed in is completely open to the elements, with no roofing and a few other facilities, and consequently audiences were clamouring for entertainment. It was not a refined Elizabethan or Jacobean theater and, if the people were unhappy with the performance, they were bombarded by every kind of grotesque missile which was why Shakespeare soon became skilled of introducing humorous and witty scenes in the aftermath of dramatic episodes so that the more "earthy" natured of the theatregoers.

Success followed SUCCESS but when Shakespeare turned 50 nearly a year following the Globe fire, his decline in health, he was forced to retire to Stratford. He was fortunate that his oldest daughter was married to the city's top physician and you are able to take a trip to "Hall's Croft", the beautiful half-timbered residence of the couple.

The good DOCTOR Hall provided his father-in law with solid advice when he advised that he should cut down on drinking and nightclubs however, it was not to be.

Chapter 7: William Shakespeare Hated To Feel Life

The curtain for Shakespeare's final performance fell quickly at the conclusion of the show following a night of partying to celebrate his youngest daughter's wedding. His entire London friends were there and, according to reports, the fervent intake of "too much Rhenish wine and pickled herrings" caused being sick the next day. More than just a hangover. Shakespeare was unable to recover despite the best efforts of John Hall to cure him, and he perished according to the legend of his 52nd birthday St George's day 1616.

The mortal remains from William Shakespeare were buried in the Stratford's Holy Trinity church, where Shakespeare's personal choices of language defy anyone to disturb him in any way:

"Good buddy", for Jesus's sake be patient,

For digging the dust contained to heare:

Bleste become the person who does not squander these stones.

Then curse be him who alters my bones."

PERHAPS his story with the loud gravediggers of Hamlet was inspired by an experience that he had personally and the notion of his skull being torn around by the cries in the form of "alas poor Shakespeare" could possibly have inspired the touching tribute.

I hope that by the end of the course of events, you'll be able to have quite different perception of Shakespeare from the one you may have begun with.

Unfortunately, thinking of the man as a cute Rogue, rather than a boring, literary giant isn't going to aid in understanding Shakespeare less difficult the first time you start however, as you advance being able to deal with a real human being who is alive and breathing and not an immovable symbol is certainly helpful. Shakespeare was not always a genius in all cases, especially when there was an important deadline to complete, and it's perfectly acceptable to criticize, as long as you support your claim.

If you're faced with a lengthy list of Shakespeare's plays it's difficult to determine the best place to begin. In fact, it's much more straightforward to determine what to stay clear of. Any person who says the idea that visiting Coriolanus could be an excellent way to get acquainted with the work that were written by William Shakespeare is probably best avoided from such a plan of action. However, for the purposes of this journal, we'll choose an alternative that is less threatening.

The majority of PEOPLE HAVE heard of Twelfth Night but as the name has no connection to the story and unless you've actually watched or read about it but you'll have no notion of what it's about. Henry IV, Richard II or as well as Macbeth as well as Romeo and Juliet provide hints that the play is likely to focus on specific individuals in the past, and, obviously when there is historical context and what the topic could be.

What is the source of Shakespeare find Twelfth Night from? The answer is very easy. The final day of Christmas festivities is Twelfth Night that falls on January 6th. that we don't really notice today since it's just thought of as the day that when we put down the Christmas decorations. But in Shakespeare's time,

Twelfth Night was if it was anything, more of a event than Christmas itself.

The Twelfth Night parties were fantastic events and the play first appeared on January 6, 1602 which is why it was given a title to Shakespeare's previously unnamed literary creation. It's easy to imagine that the ideal play to be used for an evening of celebration must be as fun and jolly as is possible which is why Twelfth Night certainly is that as it is to this day. it is a popular choice for celebrations, festivals and other events. The setting for Twelfth Night could not be more different from Elizabethan Christmastime scene, which was during the midst of an English winter.

If you take a look at the Globe Theatre, considering when this particular play actually was initially performed, it is clear that the elaborate set and effects weren't at the disposal of the company that produced it, and it was a feat of clever acting on Shakespeare's behalf in order to bring his plays to life. One might ask, whether this was achievable with a mostly uninformed audiences, but for Elizabethans who were a part of the storytelling scene, it was an extremely popular and easily accessible aspect of society and people who came to the early performances that included Twelfth Night would have been more adept at using their imagination than modern counterparts. So whenever Shakespeare declares that the play takes place in Illyria close to a beach, to the spectator it's quite as far from reality as it is possible to attain, giving them the freedom to let loose their imaginations. Furthermore, Shakespeare is also helping to pave the way for fantastic stories to develop allowing the improbable to become real in the midst of a mystical land in which the limitations of reality can be discarded throughout the story.

The most fundamental version, the plot of Twelfth Night goes like this: Orsino Duke of Illyria starts by delivering his "If music be the food of love, play on" speech. He is completely in love by the gorgeous Olivia she is trying little bit difficult to obtain, and vows to remember the passing of her father for seven years.

MEANWHILE A SHIPWRECK along of the coast of Illyria is able to separate girl and boy twins Viola as well as Sebastian. The story follows Viola and Sebastian, who believe that their brother is dead, disguises herself in a male costume for security's reasons, and then sets off to serve as a maid to Duke Orsino.

BACK at Olivia's house The fair lady's uncle sir Toby Belch is scheming to make her marry his drink lover, the handsome yet dim-witted Sir Andrew Aguecheek, but Olivia does not share her ideas.

VIOLA who is dressed in the form of an innocent boy named Cesario is in affection with Orsino however, as the Duke isn't that at all, he has none chance, especially because he's in love Olivia in the first place. Orsino is able to send Cesario in love notes to Olivia and, sure enough, Olivia falls in love with Cesario. The girl also sends Cesario the same message back to Orsino and he declines the Duke's offers however, she is her steward delightfully pompous and self-centered Malvolio pursue him by threatening him with a ring she believes he's left in his possession.

TIME for Viola to see her twin sister Sebastian and meet Sebastian, who's not even a bit deceased, after being saved by a captain of the sea named Antonio. The tale is further exaggerated because Antonio was previously involved with Orsino and both are enemies who have been sworn to. However, whenever Sebastian goes to Duke Orsino's palace in hoping for news regarding Viola, Antonio follows him.

If the mood is somewhat gloomy An element of laughter quickly puts things in a good mood. Malvolio arrives to discover Sir Toby and his pals enjoying a loud drinking party and then calls for an abrupt end to the fun. Maria the Olivia's fierce serving assistant is so enraged over Malvolio and his drunken party that she plots to win her back. Conscient of just how cute Malvolio seems, she creates his love note written by Olivia. Malvolio is enticed by it with a flutter of his fingers and is convinced Olivia as a lover of her as well as following Maria's naughty directions, which instruct him to put on white stockings and cross-garters, while laughing endlessly in the girlfriend's presence.

CHAOS ABOUNDS Olivia proclaims her affection for Cesario And Viola is averse to her sexual requests! Sir Andrew notices the two and gets in the wrong place with the stick, and asks Cesario to a fight. Malvolio is seen in a cross-dressed outfit of white stockings, smiling as a Cheshire cat, but instead of igniting Olivia's desires The object of his affection thinks that he's crazy and tells the two Sirs Toby along with Maria to keep him locked up in a room that is dark.

More confusion follows as Cesario and Andrew meet for a fight, exactly as

Antonio is about to enter. Thinking that Cesario is a friend of Sebastian He leaps into the fight and is detained by the Orsino's men, who see the man as their master's foe. But, once Viola is introduced to Sebastian, she starts to believe that her friend is alive.

SEBASTIAN appears and is misidentified as Cesario at the hands of Sir Andrew who smacks him. not knowing what's doing. Sebastian responds by giving Sir Andrew an utter beating.

OLIVIA arrives, and also mistakenly confuses Sebastian as Cesario and seduces the man into her residence before calling an unintentionally married priest their wedding.

Everything does eventually get sorted out. Sister and brother have a reunion, Olivia already has a man and when Viola discloses her identity, and confesses to her passion for Orsino and he accepts to be married. Orsino discovers Antonio is not a bad guy in the end and he releases him from the prison. Sir Toby Belch marries Maria and Malvolio gets called in after the real meaning behind the cross-gartered, inane grin comedy is exposed. You can guess that Malvolio is unable to appreciate the humorous side to the ruse and charges off and threatens a vengeful attack on the entire group.

And that's it, but as people who read this magazine, there are some things you may be interested in asking. Girls getting confused with the boys is frequently seen in Shakespeare's works which could be to be untrue for the modern audience. As for the students, just like they are all males The cast for Twelfth Night in Shakespeare's day could have been entirely masculine. Women were not allowed to perform, and keeping on the fact the fact that Viola and Sebastian were both actors of young males They would appear much more alike than one might expect to be seeing today.

ALSO Remember that Elizabethan audiences were used to tales of misidentification and especially twins in particular, and Shakespeare was certainly conscious of this. Twelfth Night had all the necessary elements for a successful box office hit and is a huge beloved with people of any age to this present day.

Even though the plot is intricate There are some hidden aspects to the characters. actually, they could had come from the pantomime. A charming lovers Orsino as well as feisty and independent Viola as well as drunken Sir Toby and beautiful Olivia and saucy Maria and a sly Malvolio each play a part and you get precisely what you will get! There is more to learn and you will find some odd hints of irony dotted along the way but ultimately Twelfth Night concerns mistaking identities and love, excellent fun or less, and is an ideal way to begin learning about Shakespeare.

Moving swiftly on Our next selection of the play is hardly distinct, and while the plot may be simple, there's plenty of depth in the characters and themes that are explored. These include first love, family conflict love, loss, and fate that ultimately lead to tragic end. It is, of course, about Shakespeare's most renowned performance, Romeo and Juliet.

Prior to THE DRAMA even begins the viewers are given a prelude, which, in its most basic form goes over the events that are scheduled to happen:

"Two Households" both identical in respectability,

Fair Verona the place where we have laid our treasures,

From a grudge-ridden past and a fresh mutiny

Civil blood can make civil hands filthy.

Chapter 8: The Fatal Legs Of The Two Enemies

Star-crossed lovers decide to take over their lives;

That misadventured smug overthrow squandered by the

In their deaths, they are buried their parents' strife.

The dreadful course of their life-long love that is marked by death,

Then the constant recurrence of their mother's anger,

That, besides at the end of their lives, they can be removed.

It is now two hours traffic on our stage;

This is if you have an open mind,

The things we'll miss the effort we put into repair."

So, right from the start, we realize that this won't be a happily ever after type of tale. The 2 "star-crossed" lovers, Romeo and Juliet have a lot to lose and we're conscious of this prior to the very first scene is even started. For students of Shakespeare there's nothing more interesting than the content of what the legendary Bard says here, but so interesting, but the way that he's saying the words!

If you count the amount of lines that are fourteen lines in all it will be clear that the prologue is one of a particular type of poetry, referred to as a sonnet. The poem has an extremely specific rhythm called iambic pentameter with a formal rhyme pattern. The sonnet is an Elizabethan sonnet, also known as a Shakespearean sonnet is how they're typically described, and of which this is the most famous illustration, rhyme abab cdcd EFEF GG.

The LAST LINES have been described as being a rhymed couplet, when you begin to experience some of the Shakespeare's words will soon be able to see that he truly was masterful of this captivating punctuational technique. In many instances, when he was trying to bring interest to one particular line or to end in a dramatic play Shakespeare often reverted to the rhyming couplet and it's important to keep a record of the words being spoken, when you encounter these. Romeo and Juliet closes with a traditional rhyming couplet, and is an excellent example to reference in your essay, because it lets readers be aware that the story will be coming to an end and the bonus is that it's easy to remember and may sound perhaps a bit corny today's ears.

"For there has never been a tale of greater angst

This is more than Juliet as well as Juliet and Romeo."

HIGH TIME and then the brief outline about Romeo as well as Juliet. It is known that there is a feud between two families in the prologue: The Montagues as well as the Capulets. In the first scene, there is an altercation in the street between two servants from the households, which spirals way out of hand when other family members join into the fight. The fight is stopped when Prince of Verona who is the ruler in the area, shows up to the scene. He swiftly declares that any more fighting among the Montagues or the Capulets could be punished with execution.

The Capulets have been hosting a celebration and we learn that Romeo who is the gorgeous young child of Lord Montague will join the celebration together with his fellow close kin Benvolio and his wonderful acquaintance Mercutio.

ROMEO'S AIM is to get acquainted with his "fair" Rosaline, a Capulet woman he imagines being in love with.

It's only possible since it's an "masked" party with everyone dressed in disguise. However, once Romeo begins to look at Juliet her mother, Lord Capulet the thought of Rosaline fade away as well "star-crossed" indeed, the innocent youngsters in Montague and Capulet are in love. When they discover their true identities There's no way to revert, and the newlywed couple is secretly married very next day.

In this moment, you might be excused for imagining that you think that the prose made a mistake and perhaps true love could be able to overcome all obstacles the odds, however Shakespeare was not so sure. It is interesting to consider that no one other than the guests could have spotted Romeo is a bit simplistic. Juliet's sister, who was a bit of a firebrand under his name Tybalt was not just spotted by Romeo in the crowd, and also pledged to pay back the injustice at every occasion.

So, when Tybalt comes across Romeo's associate Mercutio and he is it must be noted, not averse to fighting The atmosphere is high. In the moment that Romeo is about to arrive, fresh of his marriage secret with Juliet, Tybalt does everything that he can to get Tybalt into a fight. Naturally, Romeo is distracted by other matters in his head and his last desire to do is cause harm to Juliet's sister, therefore he tries to stay clear of danger. Mercutio in a state of adrenaline angry, interprets Romeo's act as cowardly, he is threatening to use his sword against Tybalt. Romeo is able to jump between them in order to stop the attack however, Tybalt is able to take advantage of this and strikes Mercutio in the fatal way while he's briefly off his security.

"A PLAGUE A BOTH YOUR HOUSES!" The victim, who to show his respect, besmirches Romeo and then seeks revenge on the murder of his companion by murdering Tybalt.

As quickly as ever The Prince is then on his way to carry his justice. Romeo has the good fortune of being exiled rather than sent to die, and solely due to the fact that Tybalt has murdered Mercutio. However, a few minutes after the wedding, Romeo and Juliet will split up.

Friar Laurence was the priest who conducted the wedding, provides whatever is possible of comfort and advises Romeo to go to neighboring Mantua in order that the raging heat will be able to calm enough for the rival families to learn of the wedding that was secret.

ROMEO and Juliet share a SINGLE intimate honeymoon with each other, but when Romeo leaves towards Mantua, Juliet is grief in a state of shock and her loving parents cause the situation to get more difficult! They believe that Juliet's sadness is because of Tybalt's passing and, to make her feel better, they suggest that she marry her Count Paris who is a nice young man who already has asked Lord Capulet to marry Juliet in wedding.

The girl who is poor can't not accept, but her parents will not accept a no response, and in desperate need of a solution Juliet looks to Friar Laurence to seek advice. He advises her to follow her parents' will, and then she is given a special potion that she can drink before the wedding. It can make her appear as if she die asleep. When she's taken to the vault of the family, Friar and Romeo are able to rescue her while the poison wears off. Once again, the hopes of the best outcome increase but are shattered by the tragedy of Shakespeare's plot!

THE LETTER that the Friar wrote for the purpose of explaining everything to Romeo disappears and Juliet's demise is the only information that reaches Romeo. In a state of suicidal despair and grief, Romeo persuades an apothecary to give him poison and then rushes to the Capulet vault, where he is taken to end his own life by his lover's right hand. At this point, nothing seems easy and the grieving the Count Paris has already arrived. Assuming that Juliet was killed due to her sorrow over Tybalt, Paris holds Romeo to be responsible for the death of his wife and blocks his entry into the vault. The two fight, Romeo is killed by Paris in a bloody battle, and then without action, Romeo discovers Juliet's "dead" body, swallows the poison, and then dies the moment Friar Laurence arrives, and Juliet is able to wake up. The priest that has discovered the dead bodies from Paris and Romeo attempts to take Juliet off quickly, but after an incident distracts him, Juliet, horrified, is stabbed in the face, rather than being in the absence of Romeo.

At this point, the Cavullets The Duke of Montague and the Prince had been brought in as the servant of Paris raised the alarm. The tragic situation before them is illogical to begin with and the responsibility falls on Friar Laurence to clarify what has occurred. The two families are shocked and recognize that it was the rift between them that led to such a tragic loss of a precious life and they come to a sense of peace in their sorrow.

There you go, the timeless love story where a one boy vying for another girl. girl and boy are in love, and when the two are separated but boy and girl again united. There's no satisfying conclusion as this reunion can only be achieved by the death process, yet it's like any other happy romance.

The characters are adapted to perform specific roles, and If you're learning about Shakespeare to pass an examination, it is possible that you will be required to look at their different roles and personalities as well. It could be beneficial to draw your own sketch-like representation of every one, including the most important points of memory.

For instance, if you look closely at Romeo it is possible to be able to describe him as uncaring and impractical. But above everything else, he is passionate. If he had been a smaller amount of impulsive, everything could have gone more easily. Romeo could have been able to walk away from the battle together with Tybalt without fear of being exiled for a few more minutes spent at the grave of Juliet and, perhaps an logical trip to Friar Laurence to learn what happened to his beloved love that was lost, and how this clever plan might work. But without his fervor, there wouldn't have been a tale to tell. And his ferocious character is the reason the public loves about him, even if it's also responsible for his personal fall.

Make sure that you define in your own terms, Juliet, Friar Laurence, Mercutio, the nurse, Benvolio, Tybalt and Paris If you can do this, then you'll be in a position to answer all questions that involve the use of characterisation in Shakespeare's play Romeo as well as Juliet. Be sure to back your thinking by quoting from the play. If you think that a particular character, like Friar Laurence, exists only to help the plot but fails to be able to stand the test of time, then it's okay to express that. Consider this: would the priest truly have Juliet's parents go through agony of believing that the death of their daughter in the event that he truly was a person of God?

On that thought-provoking note, you're ready to go to Macbeth or Macbeth, or the Scottish Play, if you are an actor with an anxiety-prone disposition.

For the reluctant Shakespeare student, Macbeth is a great favourite because it's the most concise of Shakespeare's great plays that has a simple plot, a lot in blood, gore with only a handful of main actors. It was first staged in the year 1606, most likely before the King James I. Interestingly the drama's historical context is based on Scottish descendants of King James I but the talented and shrewd Shakespeare certainly altering the facts in order to please the Royal image.

So, what's Macbeth really about? It's one of the most dramatic opening scenes in every play, with three old and ugly witches singing about their cauldrons in a storm. They plan to attack Macbeth, Thane of Glamis which the audience have yet to meet.

DUNCAN KING of Scotland has a difficult battle with the invading Vikings along with a couple of his rebellious nobles in the mix. Macbeth is a skilled soldier and loyal one, and Duncan decides to honor him with the honour as Thane of Cawdor. But, before Macbeth is aware of the news Macbeth and Banquo who is a different noble, who is loyal to King Duncan, encounter the witches while they are heading to home after fighting. Witches say that Macbeth is first going to become Thane of Cawdor before becoming King, and Banquo's kids will turn into Kings.

When Macbeth discovers he's the Thane of Cawdor He takes the witches predictions very seriously. when his wife

Macbeth, Lady Macbeth learns of the supernatural happenings and her husband is enthused, she urges him to offer the fate a hand in killing the King to get things moving faster.

WHEN DUNCAN comes in to stay over at Macbeth's castle, he's killed by Macbeth and Lady Macbeth is required to carry out the murder by covering Duncan's servants with blood before striking them with the daggers she used to kill the servants, in order that it appears as if they did the wrong thing. To prevent any questions from being posed Macbeth kills her servants likely in a fit of anger that is well-judged as Duncan's two sons, Donalblain and Malcolm run in fear for their lives when Macbeth becomes King.

PARANOIA begins to take hold and Macbeth is reminiscing about the predictions of witches, attempts to get

Banquo and his son Fleance executed. Banquo gets killed but Fleance is able to escape and, when the banquet is over, Macbeth is informed of the story the ghost of Banquo appears. He terrorizes the man!

IN DEPRETATION, MACBETH tries to find witches once more and gets an array of baffling forecasts. They advise Macbeth that he will not get hurt by someone born to a woman and that he'll be secure till Birnam Wood comes to Dunsinane. Macbeth is also warned about Macduff, who went to England to form an army to fight Macbeth which is why Macbeth is able to have each member of Macduff's family killed.

Needless to say Macduff has an extremely dim view of the situation and joins forces with Malcolm his son, who was Duncan who was killed. Duncan as they travel back to Scotland to face Macbeth. In the meantime, Lady Macbeth gets more and more crazy each day, and Macbeth is becoming increasingly lonely.

SHOWDOWN TIME and Macbeth is in Dunsinane Castle when he hears about Lady Macbeth's death while Malcolm and Macduff's forces attack the castle. However, Malcolm disguises his soldiers using tree branches from Birnam Wood and they march towards Dunsinane in fulfillment of the prophecy of the witches against Macbeth. Believing in his own strength, when he confronts the Macduff who was wronged in real life, Macbeth cries out that there is no woman born man who will hurt him. Macduff responds by saying that he came to the world via a caesarean birth, and Macbeth should be prepared for his fate. Macduff kills him. In the presence of Macbeth's head cut off, Malcolm is crowned the proper the King of Scotland.

Now, like it was with Romeo and Juliet in the past, you must know the persona, Macbeth and Lady Macbeth, Banquo, the witches, the Macduff, Duncan and Malcolm However, there is a lot to be considered about the differences. Macbeth is a story about characters that are portrayed on a psychological level. Macbeth the characters grow at a level of psychological development with themes like the power of corruption, power, good as well as evil seem to ebb and flow in accordance with the changing character. The story requires deeper thinking, and you can find a myriad of strategies to get the full knowledge of the amazing drama.

No matter what stage you're at with the course of your Shakespeare studying, make sure to discuss your work with fellow students. This will allow you to develop concepts that you may have overlooked. Many people find it useful to create an Mind Map, jotting down every thought that come up. After you've completed this, you'll be able to pull your thoughts together and arrange them into order. Find the quotes you'd like to include and then logically arrange your evidence to support your arguments.

Make sure in writing any document to lay the main points of your work within the introduction. Work through your thoughts over most of the writing during the main portion make sure you leave time for you to pull it all together in a clear concluding sentence that is well thought out and constructed. Consider it an informative, brief beginning and a strong, well-substantiated middle and an enticing short and precise conclusion. Do not ramble!

You can use these guidelines for any Shakespeare play After reading this article, you'll have lots of intriguing ideas that you can apply to the table. But, regardless of the subject you're considering, be sure to remember these important points:

First, focus to improve your character. We've had a lot of discussions about this topic and considering that Shakespeare is a master in creating fascinating and diverse characters, there's plenty of material.

Also, take a look at the plot and structure. Consider the way Shakespeare really organizes his plays and be sure you are aware of the sequence that events take place.

Do not forget the atmosphere and setting of a production. Scotland's rugged landscape, as well as the storm that occurs in which the three witches' faces are first introduced during "Macbeth" really conjure up the tense story set to unfold. Be on the lookout for shifts in scenes, and the changes in moods of the characters, as they tend to be directly connected.

Shakespeare's style of writing and usage of language is captivating and worth acquainting yourself with his most popular word play. Personification, metaphors, similes and alliteration are all well-used in his plays So, keep numerous examples of each as you're able to keep in be able to use them.

CONSIDER the point of view that each Shakespeare story is told in. What perspective is the tale presented from and what impact will that impact the viewers?

Last but not least, think about how the journal began, beginning with Shakespeare's unique story. Imagine how it could influence him as an author throughout his personal life. And remember to always think of historic events Shakespeare could have been well-aware of, in order to place the work within context.

However, with all of that said Try to keep your response and understanding of Shakespeare's plays exciting and, consequently, fresh.

Text-based commentaries and books such as they can help in focusing on a particular performance, however be aware that auditors will swiftly recognize if you've merely reprinted things you've read on the internet. Consider your ideas and come up with some creativity.

It can be difficult to believe at times, when reading a text set to a certain length, it's true that Shakespeare created plays that people could take pleasure in, solely for enjoyment. And you'll almost guarantee that there was never any test issues at the end of the performances at the Globe at the time! No one could be more astonished than Shakespeare to find modern students tackling the meanings and reasons behind his writings. This is 4000 years ago, when he first picked to his pen and parchment

And with that thought the journal comes to an end. If you were being a snob about Shakespeare it will be possible to see his work in a positive perspective, and even if you're not then at least you'll have the ability to make a compelling argument to get rid of the entire Shakespeare's works Shakespeare out of this planet.

Just remember that you're free to make your own decision regardless of what it is or to enjoy yourself or to help you pass your exam, hold with what you think is right and support your beliefs with a thorough research or quotes from the text.

It is however only right and right to Shakespeare has the final sentence on this. And in Hamlet the scene I Scene III Polonius is an older busy man, advises his son who is leaving about life, the universe, and everything. In all this lengthy ranting Shakespeare provides Polonius some wise advice to say to him, and the message should be remembered:

Chapter 9: His Entire Life

Beginning of the years

Shakespeare attended primary school in the town in Stratford in Avon and was able to study the fundamentals in Latin, Greek and French languages. The studies allowed him to study more about history as well as the classical literature. Shakespeare did not manage to finish his studies because of the poor living conditions of his father and he was forced to do. He got married (Anne Hathaway) in the year 18 and gave birth to his children (Hamnet) and an infant along with (Judith) - a daughter.

London and theatre works

He enjoyed acting, as well as poetry which led him to London and joined some of the world's most famous theatre groups and wrote their plays and published his debut poetic piece, "Venus and Adonis". It is widely regarded as among the top poets of the time and was influenced by William Shakespeare in his writings about the time of myths and kings, and in his essays concerning murder, treason and the harsh conscience. Shakespeare was inspired in his writings by the works of the historian of old Plutarch wrote.

Youth Days 1564--1585

We can now close and continue to discover to find out what the vast majority of the world is aware of about Shakespeare. Researchers are currently engaged in a focused study of the waste that Shakespeare left and studying it for the last three centuries It is crucial for us to measure the information we have gathered. There isn't that is discarded as it's not worth discussing There are questions concerning the source of every novel which are believed to be his.

No matter what it is, we're not certain of his surname. Elizabeth granted more discretion when spelling words than she allowed with her faith. Documents may contain different spelling variations for a particular word. In addition, a individual man might have signed his name with different styles according to the mood and pace of writing. So wrote his contemporaries Marlowe, Marilyn, Morley as well as others. The rest of the signatures for Shakespeare will be as follows the following: William Shakespeare-William st. Shakespeare-Wm. William Shakespeare Shakespeare This is the most popular satire today but does not be found in Shakespeare's manuscripts. The same concept.

Mary Arden, his mother Mary Arden, was born into a family of old in Workershire. Mary Arden offered John Shakespeare, the son of her father's land-tenant and a large amount of money and land. She also gave him eight children and the youngest of them was William. John gained a fortune and became a prosperous businessman within Stratford near the River Avon, bought two properties, worked for his country as an alcohol taster, the security department, an elected member of the city council, and an advisor to the officer of enforcement and generously helped people in need. However, after 1572 his assets dipped and a lawsuit was brought against him for a sum of thirty. He did not pay the fines against him and a warrant for his arrest was issued for his arrest. In 1580, for unspecified motives, he was brought before the courtroom to give a promise of not breaching security. In 1592 the name of his client was recorded in the list of people with the status of "do not attend the church on a monthly basis, according to the laws of Her Majesty." Many of them argued that the man was the type of "rebellious" Catholic, others thought the man was a Puritan as well as others stating that he was not brave enough to fight the creditors. William eventually reclaimed the money of his father as well as when his father passed away (1601) in Henley Street, only two houses remain on Henley Street in the name of Shakespeare.

The parish church of Stratford and baptized William on 16 April 1564. and Don Nicolas Roux was the first to write a biography about his life, in 1709; the story of Stratford that everyone believes has been told has it that the dad rubs his child ... during a short period of time at the school for free ... however, his difficult conditions and the desire to aid his son with his home country ... led the father to remove his son from the school (1). In his obituary, which was published in the introduction of the initial Folio Edition of Shakespeare, Ben Johnson said in his address to his adversary who passed away, "I have learned a little Latin and less Greek" .. The playwrights Greeks did not know about with respect to the Greeks to Shakespeare (not had them in sight) however, he learned sufficient Latin for him to write his tiny books with Latin fragments as well as bilingual jokes. should he have gained more knowledge from them, perhaps he would have been a scholar with active glory, in anonymity or even London became his home.

A different legend narrated in 1681 by Richard Davies about 1681 described

William Little as "was often unlucky in deer and rabbits steal, especially from Sir Thomas Lucy, who was often English whips, sometimes Asinh (2)." The 27th of November, 1582, at the time this said drunkard was just 18 years old He and Anne Hathaway, who was around twenty-five years old, were granted permission to wed. The evidence suggests that Anne's family members made it a condition for Shakespeare to get married (3). The date was May 15, 1583. After their wedding, which lasted for six months an infant was was born to two women from Omaha had a baby. Anne then poet twins with the names in the name of Hamnet or Judith on February 2nd 1585. Perhaps, at the year's end, Shakespeare abandoned his wife and his children. We don't have any data on him during 1585 and 1592.

However, we have him listed acting as a representative for London.

Chapter 10: Evolution In The Poetry 1592-1595

Shakespeare's very first quote here is a snide reference to. The 3rd of September 1592 at his funeral, Robert Green issued a message to his friends warning them who he had pushed away from the theater he was in. the London theater "A budding crow adorns our feathers, and that he is in a brutal daring (with a tiger heart) wearing the skin of actors, (and this is a stinging attack on a house in Henry play VI), and thinks that it is able to Attn hair transmitter as the best person in you. as it leads all user tasks, in his conception that the best actor in any country (4). " The text was drafted to be part of The Green Book. Green Book "is worth a few cents" of Green's intelligence. Henry Chatel, who presented his apology in the following letter. an apology addressed to the one among two individuals (and most likely Marlowe as well as Shakespeare) and apologizing to Shakespeare.

They fought them Green.

I was not connected to one of the assailants and I never be concerned about them.

and I'd not have any connection to one or the other. In the case of the other one regretfully, I realized that his actions were not pleasing, nor was it inferior in the job he claims to have, and further all the different customs prove the authenticity of his behavior and reflect his integrity and civility when writing. This confirms his talent (5).

There is there is no doubt that Greene's remark and Shuttle's apology was in reference to Shakespeare. As soon as 1592 arrived an thief from Stratford had been an actor as well as a playwright at the time in the capital. Dodal (1693) as well as Row (1709) relate his experience of being "received in the theater as a servant of a very low rank (6)" This is conceivable. His chest was filled in the most fervent desire "he was eager for the art of this and the ability of that, without his thinking deviating from anything but majesty and majesty (7)." He quickly took on small roles and made himself an enjoyable and delight to see (8) and then took on the character in the play "Adam the"

Sincere" in the novels "On Your Own" and The Ghost in Hamlet, it could have reached an even higher degree since his name was on in the cast list featured in Jonson's Everyman In His Humor or in the Jonson's Sejanus book (1604) He as well as Wuridge are "the most dramatic actors (9)". Then, in 1594, he was part of

The Chamberlain Actors. The actor did not earn his fortune writing plays instead, he was an actor, and a member of an ensemble of theater.

However, it is believed that in 1591 he was writing novels. The evidence suggests that he was as a "doctor for the novel" (treating and looking at the manuscript) and he then altered, revised and edited the writings of the group. Then he left the band to be a part of the creation of the novel. The three books in Henry VI (1592) appear to be a co-production. In the following years, he published each year two novellas, up to the point of thirty-six or 38 novels. A few of his earlier works, such as Two Gentlemen Of Venoma, Acomedy of The Errors (1594), Loves Labours Lost (1594) is a humorous wit and laughter that's now tiring for the readers. It's an important reminder that Shakespeare was able to climb the ladder of fame through perseverance and hard work. However, the climb was not easy. The novel of Marlowe "Edward II" suggested to the author that he should explore ideas within English historical literature to develop a number of theatre topics, while Richard II's story (1595) stood out from Marlowe's. Richard III (1592) had already received the title. The incident occurred in the wrong way, creating one person who was a recipe King humpback the ambition to commit treason and murder that was smuggled, however occasionally rose out of the Mtoy novel analysis Marlo and an impression of strength, as well as sparks of bright phrases. The expression "Horse! Horse! My Kingdom in exchange for a Horse!" It soon became a hit in London.

www.ingramcontent.com/pod-product-compliance
Lightning Source LLC
Chambersburg PA
CBHW070735020526
44118CB00035B/1359